To all the new lawyers embarking on this remarkable journey, may you find wisdom, resilience, and joy in every step of your legal career.

# The New Lawyer's Bible

By Taylor S. Prescott

## Contents

Introduction ..................................................................................... 7

Section 1: A Fish Out of Water: Starting Out and Finding Your Place ............................................................................................. 9

    It Gets Better, It Really Does ................................................. 10

    Treat Your Assistant Like Gold ............................................. 13

    Find a Peer Group ................................................................... 16

    Find a Mentor .......................................................................... 19

    Mastering Your Firm's Filing System and Software ......... 22

    Firm Culture ............................................................................ 24

Section 2: People You Want to Know: Building Professional Relationships ............................................................................... 27

    Networking is Important ....................................................... 28

    Build a Relationship with Court Staff ................................. 31

    Support Your Colleagues ....................................................... 33

    Staff Functions: Navigating the Minefield ......................... 36

    Treat Opposing Counsel with Respect ................................ 38

Section 3: The Business of Law: Show Me The Money ......... 41

    Billable Hours Matter ............................................................ 42

    Collected Really Matters ....................................................... 45

    Always Have a Retainer ........................................................ 48

    Don't Do Phone Consultations ............................................. 51

    Setting Goals: Process Over Destination ............................ 53

    Building Your Own Practice: Gain Power ......................... 55

Section 4: Clients: A Love/Hate Relationship ........................ 58

Picking Your Clients: The 5% Rule ..................................59

Train Your Clients..............................................................61

Manage Client Expectations: The Art of Keeping It Real .64

Find a Personal Connection with Clients .........................67

Bad Instructions ................................................................70

Talk About Fees Early and Often.......................................72

Legal Advice for Family and Friends.................................75

Section 5: Practice Management and Efficiency....................78

The Whiteboard.................................................................79

Skip Lunches Out…Within Reason ..................................81

Rip the Bandage Off: Do Your Most Difficult Tasks First 84

Bill Every Single Month ....................................................86

Keep Track of Time Concurrent with Work......................88

Staying Organized: To-Do Lists and BF Systems .............90

Pro Bono Work ..................................................................92

Screen Your Calls ..............................................................95

Manage Your Appointment Times....................................98

Section 6: Practice Tips ........................................................100

How to Deal with Difficult Opposing Counsel ...............101

Use Alternative Dispute Resolution Tools .....................104

You Will Make Mistakes…That's OK .............................107

Talk to a Practice Advisor................................................110

Listen: Really, Stop Talking So Much..............................113

Go to Court as Much as Possible.....................................116

Don't Specialize Too Early...............................................119

 Welcome to the Real World: Think Before You Act ........121

Section 7: Personal Well-Being ................................................124

 The Sphere of Crisis: Keeping Your Sanity Intact ...........125

 Guard Your Personal Time .................................................128

 Exercise, Maintain Hobbies, Eat Well ...............................131

 Reward Yourself Because Nobody Else Will ....................133

 Beware of Substance Abuse and Mental Health Issues ..136

Conclusion ................................................................................139

# Introduction

Welcome to the labyrinthine and frequently baffling world of law, where the coffee is perpetually brewing, the paperwork is forever mounting, and the sense of self-doubt is omnipresent. If you're reading this, congratulations! You've just embarked on your legal career and are likely contemplating the choices that led you here.

This book, "The New Lawyer's Bible," is your trusty guide through the initial years of legal bewilderment and beyond. Think of it as a friendly companion offering sage advice, humorous anecdotes, and the occasional shoulder to cry on (metaphorically, of course—shoulders in the legal world are often too burdened for such frivolities).

This book will cover the essential journey of starting out as a new lawyer, from feeling like a fish out of water to gaining confidence and competence. You'll learn about the importance of finding mentors, building professional relationships, and navigating the unique culture of your firm.

We'll explore the business side of law, including managing billable hours and client expectations, and the delicate balance of handling clients effectively. Additionally, we'll provide tips on practice management, from organization to prioritization, and emphasize the importance of personal well-being, reminding you to guard your personal time and maintain a healthy work-life balance.

So, buckle up, grab a cup of that perpetually brewing coffee, and let's dive into the wonderfully chaotic world of being a new lawyer. It's a wild ride, but with a bit of humor and a lot of perseverance, you'll navigate these waters just fine. Welcome to "The New Lawyer's Bible."

# Section 1: A Fish Out of Water: Starting Out and Finding Your Place

# It Gets Better, It Really Does

Welcome to the illustrious world of law, where dreams of courtroom triumphs and high-stakes negotiations quickly collide with the reality of coffee-fueled late nights and a constant state of bewilderment. Allow me to assure you: it gets better. Trust me, I've been there—wide-eyed, sleep-deprived, and questioning every life choice that led me to this career.

The first couple of years as a lawyer are akin to being thrown into the deep end of a pool filled with legal jargon, endless paperwork, and a host of new and uncomfortable situations. Picture yourself as a hapless tourist trying to navigate Tokyo without a map or a grasp of the language. Everything is strange, and you feel like a fish out of water—except the water is actually a swamp of legal documents and the fish is expected to know what a "demurrer" is.

Your office, initially a place of promise, soon becomes a maze of unfamiliar filing systems and software that appear to have been designed by a team of particularly cruel engineers. You will spend an inordinate amount of time trying to figure out how to save a document as a PDF instead of a PNG. Just when you think you've mastered it, there will be an update. Always an update.

And then there's the work itself. Each task, no matter how small, seems to take an eternity. Drafting a memo, which you were assured would take an hour or two, now consumes your entire day—and half the night. Your work hours become a blur of days blending into nights, with weekends becoming a myth akin to unicorns and the Loch Ness Monster.

You might find yourself wondering if you're just not cut out for this, if perhaps the universe made a clerical error in assigning you to the legal profession. But I can tell you, you're not alone. Every lawyer, even the ones who look like they've got it all figured out, started exactly where you are now: overwhelmed, questioning, and exhausted. It's a rite of passage.

Here's the silver lining: it does get better. There are two key milestones in this journey from feeling utterly lost to somewhat competent: the two-year mark and the five-year mark.

At around two years, something magical happens. You begin to encounter situations you've seen before. The jargon that once seemed like gibberish starts making sense. You find yourself handling tasks with a bit more confidence and a bit less panic. It's like learning to drive; at first, everything is overwhelming, but soon you're changing lanes and parallel parking with relative ease (or at least without causing a multi-car pileup).

By the five-year mark, you'll find that novel situations are the exception rather than the rule. Most days, you'll know what to do and how to do it. You'll no longer need to fake it until you make it because, well, you've made it. The feelings of being overwhelmed will fade, replaced by a sense of competence and, dare I say, occasional enjoyment.

There's no shortcut through the painful learning curve of those early years. It's a grind, but it's a grind that thousands of other new lawyers are experiencing right alongside you. So take heart, be tough, and grind on. Each meeting, each court appearance, and each memo drafted brings you one step closer to competence.

Remember, you're not stupid or ill-suited to the profession. You're simply a new lawyer, and every new lawyer goes through this. It gets better, I promise. And one day, you'll look back and laugh at the days when saving a PDF was your biggest challenge.

# Treat Your Assistant Like Gold

One of the first pearls of wisdom I received early in my career, delivered with the gravity usually reserved for presidential addresses and instructions on diffusing bombs, was this: an experienced assistant is exponentially more valuable to a law firm than a fresh-faced new associate. Think of it this way—your assistant is a proven treasure, a gem with a dazzling array of knowledge and skills, while you, dear new associate, are an unpolished and untested prospect. In the world of law, the assistant is the gold standard, and you, my friend, are a speculative venture with potential for future returns.

The takeaway here? You need to ensure you're on the good side of any assistant you work with. Picture it: strutting into the office like a hotshot lawyer barking orders left and right—this is not the way to win friends and influence people, especially not your assistant. Instead, think of yourself as an ambassador of goodwill, spreading respect and niceness wherever you go.

A seasoned assistant knows far more than you will ever know about the administrative machinations of the legal world. They are the quiet puppeteers behind the scenes, orchestrating the smooth flow of your professional life. They will free up your time to do lawyerly things—like penning impressive memos and dazzling in court—by handling the myriad of tasks that keep the office running like a well-oiled machine. From dealing with clients to ensuring your billing and collections are in pristine order, they are the unsung heroes of your success.

If you manage to alienate your assistant, you're signing up for a professional nightmare. A bad relationship with your assistant is like trying to swim with an anchor tied to your ankle—possible, but unnecessarily difficult and utterly exhausting. So, how do you avoid this pitfall?

Take them out for lunch. Buy them a small gift on their birthday and at Christmas. Show them that they are appreciated not just as an office utility but as a person. These small gestures go a long way in fostering a positive relationship. It's a simple equation: happy assistant equals happy lawyer. Trust me on this one.

One might think that the art of buttering up one's assistant is an outdated practice, something from the days when lawyers wore powdered wigs and quill pens were the height of technology. But no, this art remains as relevant today as it ever was. Your assistant is your lifeline, your support system, your backstage pass to the inner workings of the world of legal practice.

Respect them. Learn from them. Understand that their wealth of knowledge and experience is a treasure trove that can help you navigate the tricky waters of your early legal career. They will guide you, support you, and, if you play your cards right, even save you from potential blunders that could tarnish your budding reputation.

Foster a relationship built on mutual respect and appreciation. Recognize their contributions and understand that without them, your journey through the legal world would be considerably more treacherous. So, the next time you think about strutting into the office with an air of self-importance, remember this advice: be nice, be respectful, and always, always value your assistant. They are the true stars of the legal world, and you, my dear associate, would do well to remember that.

# Find a Peer Group

In my first year of practice, I found myself in a firm nestled in a small town with fewer than 20 lawyers in the entire vicinity. The most junior lawyer next to me was a 15-year call. In other words, they had been practicing law since I was fretting over middle school math. I was going through all the usual challenges of being new to the profession—imposter syndrome, long hours, baffling legal procedures—but I had nobody to commiserate with. I was adrift in a sea of seasoned veterans who seemed to have forgotten what it was like to be a greenhorn. In short, I was miserable.

This brings us to the next crucial piece of advice for any new lawyer: find a peer group. Nothing soothes the ailments that come with the practice of law more than knowing you aren't alone in the struggle. There's something incredibly therapeutic about having a good vent session, much like the emotional equivalent of a deep-tissue massage. Someone to listen to you complain about the stack of work that was dumped on your desk at 5:00 pm on a Friday, about what a jerk the judge was, and how unreasonable everything in your life has become.

Imagine sitting in your office, the clock ticking ever closer to an unholy hour, and staring at a pile of documents that seem to be breeding like rabbits. Now, imagine you have a colleague—another hapless new lawyer—who bursts into your office and says, "Can you believe this? They expect us to finish all this by Monday!" Suddenly, you're not alone. You share a laugh, maybe a cry, and a mutual understanding that you're both knee-deep in the same quagmire.

If you're lucky, you might have other junior lawyers in your firm. If not, don't despair. Join a young lawyers or young professionals group. These groups are a godsend. They organize events, provide mentorship opportunities, and, most importantly, offer a platform for you to meet others who are in the same boat. If you're in a remote area or just can't find a local group, the internet is your friend. Online forums for junior lawyers are plentiful and can be a lifeline. It's a bit like AA for new lawyers, but with fewer sad stories and more complaints about billable hours.

I cannot stress enough how vital this is for your mental health. The practice of law is demanding, stressful, and at times, downright brutal. Having a support network of peers who understand exactly what you're going through can make all the difference. It's like a secret society where everyone knows the pain of dealing with a particularly difficult client or an impossible deadline.

So, find your tribe. Seek out those who can share in your frustrations, your small victories, and your late-night rants. You'll find that these connections not only provide emotional support but also invaluable professional guidance. They can offer insights, share experiences, and even provide solutions to problems that have you stumped.

The importance of finding a peer group cannot be overstated. They will keep you sane, help you navigate the rough waters of your early career, and provide a much-needed sense of camaraderie. Remember, misery may love company, but in the world of law, it's the shared experiences and mutual support that truly make the journey bearable. Trust me—your mental health will thank you.

# Find a Mentor

When I was a junior lawyer, I was fortunate enough to have a senior lawyer in the office next to me who found me tolerable. This in itself was a small miracle, as junior lawyers can often be as bothersome as mosquitoes at a summer picnic. This senior lawyer, let's call him Bob, regularly provided me with work on his files—everything from drafting to court appearances.

Bob was a staunch believer in the power of the red pen. I would draft documents with all the earnestness of a first-year associate, only to have them returned looking like a crime scene—red ink splattered across every line, margin, and footnote. His corrections were so extensive that the pages often contained more red than black. It was humbling, to say the least, but it taught me how to draft properly.

His door was always open for questions, and trust me, I had a lot of them. Bob's mentorship was invaluable. He provided sage advice distilled from years of experience, delivered with the kind of dry humor that makes you laugh and think at the same time. A good mentor will do this—provide guidance, wisdom, and the occasional sarcastic remark to keep you grounded.

So, how do you find your own Bob? Simple. Approach a senior lawyer in your firm. Tell them you are interested in their field and offer to assist on their files. The answer will almost always be yes because, let's face it, who doesn't want free labor? If they say no, consider yourself lucky—you've just dodged a bullet because you wouldn't want to work with that individual anyway.

If there's nobody in your firm who fits the bill, don't despair. Look outside your firm. Lawyers are, despite popular belief, generally good people who enjoy imparting their hard-earned knowledge. Offer to take a potential mentor out for lunch. Trust me, free food is a universally appreciated gesture. Over sandwiches and coffee, discuss your interest in their field, and most likely, you'll find them willing to take you under their wing.

A good mentor will help you navigate those tricky situations where you have no clue what to do. They'll provide you with a safety net of experience, allowing you to take risks and grow without the fear of crashing and burning. They'll make you a better lawyer and, most likely, a better person. Over time, they'll become more than just a mentor; they'll become a friend. And you can never have too many of those.

Having a mentor means having someone to turn to when you're staring down the barrel of an impossible deadline or dealing with a particularly obstinate opposing counsel. They'll share war stories that make your current predicament seem manageable. They'll offer advice that is practical, grounded, and born of experience.

Finding a mentor is one of the best things you can do for your career. It's like having a personal GPS specifically designed for the world of law. They'll guide you, teach you, and help you become the best lawyer you can be. So go out there, find your Bob, and start soaking up all the wisdom they have to offer.

# Mastering Your Firm's Filing System and Software

The law firm filing system—exciting (not at all), bewildering, and occasionally akin to finding yourself in a maze with no cheese at the end. The sooner you get familiar with your firm's physical and digital filing systems, along with their time-keeping and document management systems, the better off you will be. Navigating these systems is like learning a new language, and fluency is key to survival.

Start with your assistant. Seriously, they are the Gandalf to your Frodo in this epic journey. Ask them to spend some time explaining the intricacies of the filing system. For physical files, this might involve color coding that looks like it was devised by a particularly imaginative preschool teacher, but it has its logic. Learn where files are kept, how a file is opened and closed, and the storage system for closed files. Is there a special dungeon for the really old ones? You need to know these things.

Next, tackle the digital realm. Digital files can be a chaotic mess or a symphony of organization. Is it uniform throughout the firm, or does each lawyer have their own eccentric system? You'll find that some lawyers organize their files with the precision of a Swiss watchmaker, while others seem to follow the "pile and pray" method. Adapt accordingly and figure out the commonalities.

Now, let's talk about software. Most lawyers use about 5% of the functionality offered by their firm's software. Imagine buying a state-of-the-art sports car and only driving it in first gear. It's a tragedy! Don't be that person. Dive into any online training available for your timekeeping and document management systems. These tools are designed to make your life easier.

Time-keeping software is your bread and butter. It's how you'll account for your billable hours, and believe me, every minute counts. Learn to use it efficiently. Set up timers, get familiar with how to log different types of work, and keep it updated in real-time.

Document management systems are another beast entirely. If you become proficient with the tools your system offers, you'll not only be more productive, but you'll also gain valuable insights into your practice. You'll be able to retrieve documents faster, manage your workload better, and even automate some of the mundane tasks that suck the joy out of your day.

Invest the time to learn your firm's filing system and software. It may seem tedious at first, but the payoff is immense.. So, roll up your sleeves, dive into the training modules, and embrace your inner tech geek.

# Firm Culture

Firm culture—a term that conjures images of everything from toga parties to solemn gatherings reminiscent of a Victorian funeral. Believe me, firm culture is a real thing, and it can vary wildly from one firm to the next. Some firms are the legal world's equivalent of a frat house, with a full keg on tap in the office (yes, seriously) and Friday nights turning into epic drunk-fests that don't end until the wee hours of Saturday. Others resemble a family picnic, where many lawyers and staff have young families, and the firm hosts summer BBQs complete with a clown show and a bouncy castle. Then there are the gladiatorial firms, where associates (and their billable hours) are pitted against each other in a Darwinian struggle for partnership.

Ideally, you will have scoped out your firm's culture before you signed on the dotted line, making it part of your decision-making process. But let's face it, sometimes you're so dazzled by the offer that you overlook the finer details. If you didn't know what your new firm's culture was before you started, don't worry—you will within days. It's hard to miss when your colleagues are doing keg stands in the break room or organizing a bake sale for the local school.

Fitting into your firm's culture is crucial because it means you share similar values and priorities with your colleagues. This shared ethos makes life infinitely easier. Imagine trying to fit a square peg into a round hole—it's awkward, frustrating, and ultimately, it just doesn't work. If you're at a party firm but prefer quiet nights with a good book, you're going to feel like a cat in a dog park. Conversely, if you thrive on competition but find yourself at a laid-back, family-oriented firm, you might end up feeling like a greyhound in a room full of pugs.

If you don't fit into your firm's culture, you run the risk of feeling isolated and becoming a silo within the firm. That, my friend, is no bueno. Isolation can lead to a lack of camaraderie, support, and ultimately, job satisfaction. You might find yourself dreading Monday mornings more than usual, and that's a slippery slope to burnout.

Should you find yourself completely at odds with your firm's culture, my recommendation is to tough it out for a year or two, gain some valuable experience, and then look to make a change to a firm that fits your personality better. Think of it as dating—sometimes you have to kiss a few frogs to find your prince or princess. There's no shame in admitting that a particular firm isn't the right fit for you. In fact, recognizing this and acting on it shows a level of self-awareness and courage that will serve you well throughout your career.

In the meantime, try to find common ground with your colleagues. Participate in firm events, even if they're not exactly your cup of tea. Who knows? You might find that you actually enjoy the occasional office party or family picnic. And if not, at least you'll have some entertaining stories to tell.

Firm culture is an essential aspect of your professional life. It affects your job satisfaction, your relationships with colleagues, and ultimately, your career trajectory. So, take the time to understand and evaluate the culture of any firm you're considering. And if you find yourself in the wrong place, don't be afraid to make a change. After all, life's too short to be anything but happy in your work.

# Section 2: People You Want to Know: Building Professional Relationships

# Networking is Important

If you are anything like me, there is nothing more dreadful than eating bad food and having an awkward conversation with someone you've just met. Some people seem to thrive on this sort of thing, gliding effortlessly from one bland canapé to the next, while seamlessly chatting up strangers as if they were lifelong friends. For me, however, this is pure torture. But—and it pains me to say this—networking is necessary if you want to excel as a lawyer.

Done properly, networking will eventually bless you with a circle of contacts that keep work flowing in your direction and provide assistance in areas where you're not exactly a wizard. Think accountants, financial planners, and real estate agents. So yes, you do need to network. But the key to making it bearable is to find what you enjoy.

For instance, I loathed the pervasive wine-and-cheese events that are foisted upon so many lawyers. The idea of balancing a glass of Merlot while pretending to enjoy a piece of rubbery Brie was enough to make me consider a career change. So, I took a different approach. I held a monthly poker tournament at my firm instead. I would invite 10 to 15 people I thought would make good contacts, and we'd play a fun two hours of poker and eat pizza. This eliminated the awkward small talk because, let's face it, there's always something to discuss when you're bluffing your way through a hand of Texas Hold'em. The people who attended enjoyed the tournaments as well, and even began hosting their own tournaments.

Another thing to remember is that networking doesn't need to be labeled as such. Your young lawyer group is networking, even if all you do is get together and party once a month. I once had a lawyer hand over her entire practice to me when she decided to take time off to be with her family more. How did I meet her? Through a young lawyer group whose primary function was to go to the bar together once a month. We bonded over cocktails and bad karaoke, and when the time came for her to step away, she remembered me.

The beauty of networking is that it doesn't have to be a formal, stilted affair. Find something you enjoy and turn it into a networking opportunity. Love hiking? Start a hiking club and invite other professionals. Enjoy cooking? Host a dinner party where each guest brings a dish. The possibilities are endless, and the key is to make it enjoyable for yourself. After all, if you're having fun, it won't feel like networking—it'll just feel like socializing.

Networking is important, but it doesn't have to be dreadful. By finding ways to incorporate it into activities you actually enjoy, you'll build a network of valuable contacts without the awkwardness and bad food. Think outside the box and find a networking style that doesn't suck. Trust me, your career will thank you.

# Build a Relationship with Court Staff

One of the recurring themes you'll find running through this book is the importance of treating people well. Whether it's your assistant, your colleagues, or your clients, being pleasant, respectful, and occasionally funny can work wonders. This is especially true when it comes to court staff. These folks are the guardians of the courthouse, and let me tell you, making friends with them can be the secret sauce to a smoother legal career.

Court staff can be a bit like a rabid pitbull that skipped breakfast—they can seem grumpy, unapproachable, and downright mean at times. But here's the thing: you should always be courteous and pleasant with them. Seriously, say hello to the court clerk and thank him or her for their time at the end of the day. Tell the registry staff that you really appreciate how quickly they handled your filings. It's not just good manners; it's strategic.

Imagine you're in a rush to file an important document, and the clock is ticking ominously towards the deadline. You sprint to the filing counter, only to find it closed. But wait! The court staff recognizes you—the same person who brought them donuts last Christmas and always has a kind word. They decide to bend the rules a bit, opening the counter for a few precious minutes to let you file.

The benefits don't stop there. When you're on good terms with court staff, they might be more willing to offer a courtesy correction on a document with an error. Imagine catching a mistake before it becomes a problem just because the clerk decided to give you a heads-up. Or think about the clerk who decides to be a little less stern with you because you always make an effort to be polite. These little moments add up, making your professional life that much easier.

Let's not forget the simple power of appreciation. A thank you here, a compliment there, and perhaps a big box of chocolates or donuts during the holidays can go a long way. It's a small investment with potentially big returns. And really, who doesn't appreciate a good donut?

Building a relationship with court staff is simply a wise career move. Treat them well, and you'll find your path a bit less treacherous. They'll remember you as the lawyer who was always courteous, who always had a kind word, and who brought those amazing donuts last Christmas. So go ahead, be the lawyer who brightens their day. Trust me, it will brighten yours as well.

# Support Your Colleagues

Being a lawyer can sometimes feel like being trapped in a pressure cooker with the lid firmly sealed. Deadlines are always looming, clients are perpetually demanding, and sometimes you forget something as crucial as your tie on the day of a big court appearance. It's in these moments of crisis that the true value of supporting your colleagues becomes glaringly apparent.

Imagine it's Monday morning, and you're running on nothing but caffeine and sheer willpower. Your deadline for a massive case is hurtling towards you like a freight train, and you've hit a brick wall in your research. You look over and see your colleague, Jane, who seems to be calmly navigating her own sea of legal paperwork. In this moment of desperation, you might think it's best to suffer in silence, but that would be a rookie mistake. Lawyers, especially junior ones, need to stick together.

Now, imagine Jane notices your plight. She remembers her own moments of panic when deadlines felt like doomsday clocks and legal problems seemed insurmountable. She decides to help. Jane spends a few hours helping you research case law, sharing advice on how she solved a similar problem last month. This isn't just camaraderie; it's survival.

Supporting your colleagues in their time of need is not just the right thing to do as a decent human being, but it's also a savvy career move. The legal profession is demanding, and the stress can be intense. By helping each other, you create a safety net that ensures no one has to face the challenges alone. It's a bit like forming an impromptu superhero team, with each member ready to leap into action when another is in distress.

Think of it as building up good karma within the firm. When you step in to help a colleague, you're investing in a future where they'll do the same for you. And let's be honest, your moment of crisis is coming. Perhaps it'll be an all-nighter prepping for a trial, or a tech disaster right before a crucial presentation. When that day comes, you'll be thankful for the network of supportive colleagues you've cultivated.

So, next time you see a colleague drowning in a sea of case files or frantically searching for a missing tie, step up. Spend a few hours helping them research, offer advice from your own experiences, or find someone who can provide the guidance they need. Your small acts of kindness will foster a supportive work environment and build strong professional relationships.

Supporting your colleagues is about more than just lending a hand; it's about creating a resilient, cooperative workplace where everyone thrives. Your acts of kindness and support will be repaid when you need them most, making your journey through the legal profession a little less daunting and a lot more rewarding. Be the colleague who steps in, lends a tie, and saves the day. You'll be better for it, and so will your firm.

# Staff Functions: Navigating the Minefield

Staff functions—two words that can strike fear into the heart of even the most seasoned lawyer. Sometimes, they're a blast, but let's be honest, they often feel like one more obligation on an ever-growing list of obligations. Yet, despite the soccer game you're missing or the fact that your spouse is sick of you getting home past midnight, you need to go. You need to smile. You need to be social.

Think of staff functions as a necessary evil, like flossing your teeth or filing your taxes. The trick is to change your mindset: instead of viewing them as a chore, see them as an opportunity. It's a chance to get to know the lawyers or staff you don't work directly with. Expanding your network within the firm can pay off in unexpected ways, from discovering new allies to finding mentors who can help you navigate your legal career.

Now, let's talk about the art of being social without being a spectacle. You want to be memorable, but for the right reasons. First and foremost, have a drink or two if it helps you relax, but—and this is crucial—do not get drunk. You don't want to be the person grinding against the senior partner on the dance floor or vomiting in the limo home and having to send the firm-wide apology email the next day. Instead, share a funny anecdote, laugh at others' jokes, and remember to listen more than you speak. People love to talk about themselves, and being a good listener is a surefire way to win friends.

As the evening wears on, you'll likely find yourself getting more comfortable. This is when you might be tempted to let loose a bit. Resist this urge. Remember, everything you do at a staff function will be remembered and possibly recounted in excruciating detail at the office the next day, the next month, and the next year. Keep it professional, keep it light, and, for heaven's sake, keep your dignity intact.

By the end of the night, you'll have hopefully made some new connections, strengthened existing ones, and perhaps even enjoyed yourself a little. As you head home (sober, I hope), pat yourself on the back. You've survived another staff function and emerged unscathed.

Staff functions are an essential part of your professional life. They may seem like a nuisance, but they're valuable opportunities to expand your network and build relationships within the firm. Approach them with a positive attitude, a strategic plan, and a commitment to keeping it classy.

# Treat Opposing Counsel with Respect

In the thrilling, fast-paced world of law, it's easy to get caught up in the heat of the moment. You're vigorously representing your client, heart pounding, adrenaline pumping, and suddenly, opposing counsel becomes the enemy. It's like a courtroom version of "Game of Thrones," and you're ready to draw swords. But wait—before you go full gladiator, let's take a step back and remember something crucial: every opposing counsel is your colleague, dealing with the same pressures, deadlines, and client expectations as you are.

The dispute between your respective clients is not a personal grudge match between you and the other lawyer. It's essential to keep this perspective. Treat the other lawyer with the same respect you expect to be treated with, even when they seem determined to test the limits of your patience. I know, I know—it's tempting to respond to a snarky email with an equally snarky retort. Resist this urge. Take the high road. Channel your inner diplomat.

Here's the thing: treating opposing counsel with respect has a multitude of benefits that go beyond mere professional courtesy. First and foremost, you'll build a reputation for being someone who is good to deal with. This reputation will follow you throughout your career, making interactions smoother and less contentious. Lawyers talk, and being known as a respectful and reasonable attorney can open doors and create opportunities you might not expect.

Some of these opposing counsels will become friends over the years as you work with them on multiple occasions. You'll share war stories, commiserate over difficult clients, and perhaps even enjoy the occasional drink together. These relationships can be invaluable. You'll find that a friend in the profession is a treasure of advice and support.

Here's another perk of treating opposing counsel with respect. Lawyers often refer cases to other lawyers they trust and respect. If you've built a reputation for being tough but fair, reasonable, and pleasant to work with, don't be surprised if you start getting referrals from lawyers you've gone up against. They'll remember you as someone who made a tough situation more manageable, and that's gold in the legal world.

So, how do you do this? Start with the basics: be polite in your communications, whether they're in person, over the phone, or via email. Avoid the temptation to get personal or petty. If a negotiation gets heated, take a deep breath and remember that it's not about winning against the other lawyer—it's about achieving the best possible outcome for your client. And always, always follow through on your commitments. If you say you'll do something, do it. Reliability breeds respect.

Treating opposing counsel with respect is not just about being a decent human being (although that's a pretty good reason on its own). It's a strategic move that can make your professional life easier, more pleasant, and more successful. You'll build a strong reputation, create valuable professional relationships, and make your job a little less stressful. So, sheath your sword, extend a hand, and treat your opposing counsel with the respect they deserve.

# Section 3: The Business of Law: Show Me The Money

# Billable Hours Matter

Ah, the joy of tracking your life in six-minute increments! If that sentence made you groan inwardly, welcome to your new world. As much as it pains us all, this is how most lawyers keep track of their time. And for junior lawyers, it's especially crucial. This little exercise in time-slicing will be a major component of how your firm evaluates you. Sure, being nice, being a team player, and producing quality work are important, but let's not kid ourselves—the number of hours billed reigns supreme.

Think of your billable hours as the heartbeat of your legal career. Without them, you're not just out of sync; you're flatlining. Your billable hours will determine everything from your year-end bonus to your overall standing in the firm. Produce enough of them, and you're a star. Fall short, and you might find yourself spending the holidays catching up in an empty office, or worse, looking for a new job.

Here's a tip: get comfortable with the math. Figure out what you need to bill every day to hit your target for the year, taking into account holidays, weekends, and the occasional sick day. If your annual goal is 2,000 hours, that breaks down to roughly 40 hours a week, or about 8 billable hours a day if you take no vacation (which I don't recommend).

Now, a word about non-billable hours and pro-bono work. In my first five years of practice, I diligently tracked these hours along with my billable ones, like a good little soldier. Did they matter in my annual evaluations? Not that I could tell. I've heard mythical tales of firms where these hours actually count, but I've yet to meet anyone who's worked at one of these unicorn firms. Don't treat these hours as equal to billable hours – they aren't.

The key to success here is simple: stay on top of your billable hours. It's easy to let them slip, telling yourself you'll catch up next week. But before you know it, you're staring down the barrel of a holiday season spent chained to your desk, while your friends and family are off enjoying eggnog and New Year's parties. Don't be that person.

Here's how to avoid this grim fate. Make a plan and stick to it. Aim to exceed your daily target slightly, so you have a buffer for those days when everything goes wrong, or when the allure of a sunny afternoon proves irresistible. And for heaven's sake, don't procrastinate. Time management apps, sticky notes, whatever it takes—use them.

Also, be realistic about how you spend your time. Not every moment at the office is billable. There's the meals out, coffee breaks, the chit-chat by the water cooler, and the endless parade of firm meetings. Be mindful of these time sinks and try to reduce them as much as possible.

Tracking your life in six-minute increments is a pain, but it's a necessary one. Your billable hours are the metric by which you'll be judged, rewarded, and ultimately succeed. Stay ahead of the game, and you'll not only survive but thrive. And remember, when the clock strikes midnight on New Year's Eve, you want to be holding a glass of champagne, not a stack of files.

# Collected Really Matters

The difference between billable and collected can be the fine line between success and sleepless nights. As a new lawyer, you'll quickly learn that while billable hours are important, the real magic happens when those hours transform into collected dollars.

In your first year or two, you won't have much control over your collected number, also known as dollars in the door. Most files you work on will belong to other lawyers, and they'll be in charge of the billing on those files and applying any discounts or time write-offs. It's a bit like being a sous chef in a bustling kitchen—you do a lot of the chopping and stirring, but the head chef gets the credit (and the paycheck). Expect your time to be written off to some extent at the beginning. After all, the senior lawyer won't want to charge the client for the 12 hours it took you to draft a simple memo that should have taken three. This is normal.

But as your career progresses, things change. You'll start taking on your own clients and managing your own files. Suddenly, those billable hours need to turn into cold, hard cash and it's your responsibility. Your firm isn't just interested in how many hours you've billed; they want to see those hours reflected in the bank account. There will come a time when your collected figure is significantly more important than your billable hours.

So, how do you make sure you get paid for all those hours you've worked? Start making it a practice from the beginning to ensure that any bills you have control of are paid promptly. Think of yourself as a polite but persistent debt collector. Send out invoices on time, follow up with clients, and keep track of any outstanding bills. It might feel awkward at first, but remember, you've earned that money.

Here's a little secret: the best lawyers aren't just good at practicing law; they're also great at getting paid for it. Develop a system for following up on accounts receivable. Set reminders to check in with clients about unpaid invoices, and don't be afraid to give them a gentle nudge. Most clients appreciate a reminder—it's easy for invoices to get lost in the shuffle, and a friendly follow-up can often be the difference between getting paid and being forgotten.

Also, be clear and transparent with your clients from the get-go about your billing practices. Explain how you track your time, how often they can expect invoices, and what the payment terms are. Setting these expectations early can prevent a lot of headaches down the road. Remember, your time is valuable, and you deserve to be compensated for it.

In conclusion, while billable hours are essential, collected dollars are what keep the lights on and the coffee machine running. Start developing good billing habits early, stay on top of your accounts receivable, and turn those billable hours into collected cash. Your bank account will thank you.

# Always Have a Retainer

One of the most important pieces of advice I can offer you as a new lawyer is this: always have a retainer. Think of it as your financial security blanket, your insurance policy against the whims of your clients. The work you do as a lawyer is challenging, demanding not just of your headspace but also of your precious time. The last thing you want is to do that work for free.

First, let's break down why having a retainer is so crucial. The simple truth is that clients can be unpredictable. Even the most well-meaning ones might find themselves in a position where they can't pay your bill. Perhaps they think your fees are too high (how dare they!), maybe they didn't like the results (despite your heroic efforts), or perhaps they simply don't have the funds. Whatever the reason, a retainer ensures that you get paid for the work you've done.

Imagine you've just spent a sleepless night drafting a complex motion. Your brain is fried, your coffee consumption has reached dangerous levels, and you can barely remember what day it is. The last thing you need is to find out that your client isn't going to pay for that motion. That's where the retainer comes in. It's the buffer that ensures you're compensated for your sleepless nights and caffeine-fueled efforts.

This is how I think of it - if I'm not going to get paid for the time I spend on a client's matter, I would much rather use that time doing something enjoyable, like spending it with family or friends. Watching paint dry, knitting, or even staring at the wall suddenly seem like much better options than working for free. In other words, make sure you're securing your earnings upfront.

Here's how you do it: always have a retainer agreement and a retainer in place. A well-drafted retainer agreement sets clear expectations for both you and your client. It specifies how much they need to pay upfront, what services you'll provide, and what happens when the retainer is depleted. This clarity helps prevent misunderstandings and ensures you're not left holding the short end of the financial stick.

The retainer is payment of funds that will be held in trust until work is billed. It is then transferred to your firm as revenue. When the retainer runs out, get another retainer. It's a simple yet effective system.

Now, what if a client's retainer runs dry and they're hesitating to replenish it? This is where you need to put on your firm-yet-fair hat. If a client has an outstanding balance or is refusing to provide a new retainer, you should stop working on their file unless there are arrangements in place that you and your bosses find acceptable. It's not just about protecting your own interests; it's about maintaining the financial health of the firm.

Always having a retainer is about safeguarding your time and ensuring you get paid for the hard work you do. Don't fall into the trap of working for free because a client couldn't or wouldn't pay. Make sure you're protected from the get-go with a solid retainer agreement. Your future self will thank you when you're enjoying a relaxing evening with friends instead of chasing after unpaid bills.

# Don't Do Phone Consultations

Everyone loves a freebie, and potential clients are no exception. The idea of getting legal advice for free is like catnip to them. But here's the thing, dear new lawyer: your time is valuable. You've spent years honing your skills, burning the midnight oil, and sacrificing your social life to become the legal eagle you are today. Giving away your expertise for free, especially over the phone is a fast track to frustration and financial shortfall.

Let's paint a picture here. You're at your desk, trying to wade through the mountain of paperwork that seems to have magically multiplied overnight. The phone rings. It's a potential client with a "quick question." You figure, why not? A quick chat couldn't hurt. But as you start to delve into their issue, you realize this isn't a quick question. It's a Pandora's box of legal woes, and before you know it, the "quick chat" has eaten up an hour of your precious time.

Now, if this were a paid consultation, you'd be nodding along, diligently taking notes, and thinking about what a great lunch you'll have with the fee. But it's not. It's free. And here's the kicker: they'll likely call you again for "just a bit more advice" and you'll be stuck in an endless cycle of pro bono purgatory.

Existing clients, on the other hand, are perfectly fine to speak with on the phone. They're already in the system, they're used to your billing practices, and they understand that your time is money. They're calling to continue an ongoing relationship, not to get something for nothing.

To sum up, don't do phone consultations. Guard your time like a dragon guards its treasure. Your expertise is your most valuable asset, and it deserves to be compensated. By setting this boundary early in your career, you'll save yourself a lot of headaches and ensure that your time is spent wisely—and profitably.

So, the next time the phone rings and it's a potential client asking for "just a minute" of your time, remember this advice. Politely inform them that you'd be happy to schedule a proper consultation, and that your time, like theirs, is valuable.

# Setting Goals: Process Over Destination

Setting goals is a wonderful exercise, a bit like dreaming about winning the lottery but with a slightly better chance of success. It gives you that extra bit of motivation when you need it most, like a shot of espresso for your career. But here's the thing about goals: they can be tricky little devils. Too often, people set goals that are grand and glorious but fail to capture the gritty reality of what it takes to actually achieve them. That's why I recommend focusing on the process rather than the destination.

Let's start with an example. Say your goal is to become a partner at your firm. It's a worthy goal, no doubt about it. But if you just fixate on that shiny title, you're likely to feel overwhelmed, like a mouse staring up at Mount Everest. Instead, break that goal down to the granular level. Ask yourself: what is needed to achieve this?

First, you need to meet or exceed your annual billable hour target. So, set a daily billable hour target and stick to it like glue. Next, you need to be on good terms with the existing partners. Set a goal to get face time with the partners whenever the opportunity presents itself. Finally, you need to have a book of business of your own. Set a goal to make one good contact each week.

By breaking your overarching goal into these smaller, manageable steps, you keep yourself focused on a daily, weekly, and monthly basis. Instead of looking back at the year and realizing you haven't made any progress, you'll see steady, measurable advancement toward your ultimate goal.

Another advantage of this process-oriented approach is that it keeps you flexible. If you hit a snag—say, your billable hours dip during a particularly tough month—you can adjust your daily targets to compensate. If one partner seems unapproachable, you can focus on building relationships with others. The process becomes a series of small, achievable tasks rather than one daunting monolith.

Setting goals is not just about dreaming big; it's about laying out a clear, actionable path to achieve those dreams. Focus on the process over the destination. Break your goals down into daily and weekly tasks that keep you moving forward. This way, you'll stay motivated, make consistent progress, and ultimately, find yourself standing at the summit of your own personal Everest.

# Building Your Own Practice: Gain Power

The start of your legal career is a bit like being the new kid in school, except instead of dodging dodgeballs, you're navigating a maze of briefs, billable hours, and partner expectations. At this stage, you'll primarily be working on other lawyers' files, contributing to their success while you learn the ropes. But here's a piece of sage advice: start taking steps toward building your own book of business early on. Trust me, having your own clients is like holding the keys to your own future.

At first, it might seem like building your own practice is a Herculean task. But let's break it down. Building your own book of business means gradually cultivating your own clients, the lifeblood of your professional independence. Think of it as planting a garden. You start with a few seeds, nurture them carefully, and over time, they grow into a lush, thriving garden. And who doesn't want a garden?

Having your own book of business gives you power within your firm. When you generate your own revenue, you're not just an associate; you're a rainmaker. Partners will take notice. They'll want to lock you—and your clients—into the firm via partnership. After all, who doesn't want to keep a golden goose around?

Moreover, having your own clients provides you with options. The legal world is unpredictable. Firms merge, partners retire, and office politics can sometimes resemble a Shakespearean drama. When you have your own book of business, you're not reliant on others for your income. You have the freedom to explore opportunities without the fear of losing your livelihood.

Let's say partnership is your goal. Existing partners will be much more eager to welcome you into their exclusive club if you come with your own client base. You'll be seen not just as a capable lawyer but as a valuable fee-generating asset. And if you ever decide that it's time for a change of scenery, having your own clients makes you a hot commodity. Other firms will be keen to bring you—and your stable of clients—on board. It's the legal world's version of being a free agent, with teams vying for your signature.

But the benefits don't stop there. A mature, mobile practice makes starting your own firm much, much easier. If the entrepreneurial bug bites you, having your own clients means you can hit the ground running. You won't be starting from scratch; you'll have a solid foundation on which to build your new venture. Options are never a bad thing, and building your own practice ensures you have plenty of them.

So, how do you go about this? Start by nurturing relationships. Attend networking events, join professional groups, and stay in touch with your law school classmates. Offer exceptional service to your clients, and don't be shy about asking for referrals. Over time, these efforts will pay off, and you'll find your own client base growing steadily.

Building your own practice is an investment in your future. It gives you power, independence, and flexibility. It removes your reliance on others for your income and opens up a world of opportunities. And remember, in the world of law, being the one who holds the keys to your future is the ultimate power move.

# Section 4: Clients: A Love/Hate Relationship

# Picking Your Clients: The 5% Rule

There is an allure to a new client walking through the door, check book in hand, ready to hand over a retainer like a knight presenting a gift to the queen. As a junior lawyer, it's tempting to accept every client who shows up, thinking that more clients mean more billable hours and, ultimately, more money. But let me share a nugget of wisdom that could save you countless headaches: not all clients are created equal. Enter the 5% Rule—5% of your clients will be the source of 95% of your problems.

Think of your initial consultation with every potential client as a first date. You're not just there to impress them; they're auditioning for the role of your client. Look for red flags that scream "trouble ahead." Are you their fifth lawyer? That's a big, flashing neon sign that this client might be more trouble than they're worth. Are they trying to haggle over your hourly rate as if they're at a flea market? That's another warning sign. Are they trying to dictate how their case should be run? Are they interrupting you like a hyperactive game show contestant? Are they combative or obviously lying? And, most importantly, are they disrespectful? If you answer "yes" to any of these questions, it's a signal from the Law Gods that you may want to politely decline their business.

The last thing you want is a client who constantly argues about your bills, provides terrible instructions, or is shady AF. These clients will give you more grief than a week-old hangover and will consume far more of your time than any client should. They are the proverbial bad apples, and they can spoil your entire practice if you're not careful.

If you don't catch these red flags at the beginning, don't be afraid to fire them as clients once you've caught on to their dubious ways. Yes, you heard me right—fire your clients. It may feel awkward, like breaking up with someone via text, but it's necessary. You want clients who listen to your advice, pay their bills, and, most importantly, appreciate you. Anything less is unacceptable.

Resist the temptation to take on every client who walks through your door. Remember the 5% Rule and be selective. Think of it this way: you're not just building a clientele; you're curating a group of people who respect you and your work. So, be the discerning lawyer who chooses clients wisely. It's your practice, your reputation, and your life. Choose wisely, and you'll avoid the 95% of headaches caused by that troublesome 5%.

# Train Your Clients

Let's talk about one of the most important, yet often overlooked, aspects of legal practice: training your clients. Just as you might train a puppy not to chew on your shoes, you need to train your clients to respect your boundaries and follow the rules you set. It sounds simple, but trust me, it can be as challenging as herding cats.

First things first: set the ground rules early and stick to them. Imagine you're laying the foundation for a house. If the foundation is shaky, the whole structure is doomed to collapse. Similarly, if your clients don't understand your expectations from the get-go, your professional relationship is bound to be a mess.

Let's start with money—always a touchy subject. Make it crystal clear that you expect retainers to be topped up when needed and any amounts owing to be paid promptly. Think of it like a prepaid phone plan: no top-up, no service. If clients know you're serious about this, they're more likely to respect it.

Now, onto communication. In an age where people expect instant responses, it's crucial to set boundaries about when and how you can be contacted. Don't respond to late-night emails or agree to after-hours or weekend meetings unless the situation absolutely requires it. If you do, you're essentially training your clients to think that late-night conversations and weekend appointments are perfectly normal and that you're available 24/7. Next thing you know, you'll be getting calls at 11 PM on a Saturday about a minor clause in a contract.

Imagine having a lovely dinner with friends, the wine is flowing, and your phone buzzes. It's a client, wanting to discuss their case right then and there. If you've trained your clients properly, this scenario should be as rare as a solar eclipse. Instead, set the expectation that calls and emails will be returned during business hours. Unless it's an urgent matter, most things can wait until Monday morning.

As much as possible, clients should make an appointment to speak with you. Random calls from clients should not be the norm unless there's an emergency. Make it clear that while you're dedicated to their case, you also need time to focus on other clients and, heaven forbid, have a life outside of work. Constant interruptions make it impossible to maintain focus and get work done effectively.

Let's not forget the importance of maintaining boundaries. This isn't just for your benefit—it's for your clients too. By setting clear boundaries, you're teaching them to respect your time and the time you dedicate to their case. It's a win-win situation: you get to have a balanced work-life ratio, and they receive a more focused and efficient lawyer.

Training your clients is essential for maintaining a healthy work-life balance and running an efficient practice. Set the ground rules early, be consistent in enforcing them, and don't be afraid to remind clients of these boundaries when necessary. Remember, you're not just a lawyer; you're a human being with a life outside of work. By establishing and maintaining these boundaries, you'll ensure that both you and your clients have a smoother, more productive relationship.

# Manage Client Expectations: The Art of Keeping It Real

Ah, the wonderful world of client expectations—where every client thinks they are a saint, their case is a slam dunk, and the opposition is the embodiment of evil. Clients usually have an overly positive opinion of their position in a legal matter. They're always in the right, there's no way they could lose in court, and they are the heroes of their own stories. Now, combine this with our natural instinct to say things that make people happy: "Yes, you will for sure win this case!" Sounds like a recipe for disaster, doesn't it? Well, it is.

Let's step back and give our heads a collective shake. As a new lawyer, one of the most crucial skills you can develop is managing client expectations. This starts with giving your clients an honest assessment of their case as early as possible. And by honest, I mean brutally honest, with all the warts and wrinkles included. Clients need to understand that in the world of law, there are no certainties—only a range of possible outcomes, some of which might be downright unpleasant.

Imagine your client walks into your office, full of confidence that their case is airtight. They expect you to nod in agreement and confirm their belief that victory is assured. Instead of feeding into this delusion, take a deep breath and explain the reality. Outline the best-case scenario, the worst-case scenario, and everything in between. And while you're at it, make sure to include your fees in your assessment. For example: "Your best-case scenario at trial is $100,000, but it will cost you $80,000 to get there."

Be clear that there are no guarantees in law. Every case has its risks, and some of those risks might not work out in their favor. This might not make them happy in the moment, but it will prepare them for the rollercoaster ride ahead. If you set realistic expectations from the start, you'll save both yourself and your client a lot of heartache down the line.

Now, let's address the elephant in the room: losing a case or obtaining a subjectively poor result for a client. It's going to happen. No matter how brilliant you are, not every case will end in victory. And if you've spent months reassuring your client that they can't possibly lose, they will be furious when the verdict doesn't go their way. Much angrier than if you had prepared them from day one for the possibility of an unfavorable outcome.

By managing expectations, you're not just protecting your client's emotional well-being; you're also protecting yourself. If a client feels blindsided by a loss or a less-than-stellar result, they might accuse you of not providing good advice. But if you've been upfront about the risks and potential outcomes, they're less likely to place the blame on your shoulders.

Managing client expectations is about honesty, transparency, and a little bit of tough love. Set the stage early, and make sure your clients understand that the legal process is unpredictable and often complex. Prepare them for any eventuality, and you'll find that even if things don't go their way, they'll respect you for your candor and professionalism.

# Find a Personal Connection with Clients

Clients are the bread and butter of our profession, and occasionally, the source of our migraines. A golden principle in the legal field is that having your clients like you will cover up any manner of sins. Believe me, if they think you're a decent human being rather than just a legal bill generator, you're in a good spot. The easiest way to have clients think of you as a pretty okay person is to find common interests and build a personal connection.

Start by gathering intel. No, you don't need to go full detective mode, but do find out a bit about them. Do they have kids? Who are their favorite sports teams? Where did they last go on holiday? What are their hobbies? Keep a list of these interests if your memory isn't quite up to Sherlock Holmes' standards. This small effort can pay huge dividends in the long run.

When you meet with clients, start off with a few minutes of casual conversation about these interests. It's a bit like warming up before a workout. Don't dive straight into the legal jargon and heavy stuff right away. Ease into it. For example, if you know they're a die-hard fan of the local football team, start with, "Did you catch the game last night? What a finish!" They'll light up, and suddenly, you're not just their lawyer; you're a fellow human being who shares their passion for football.

This approach works wonders over time. Clients will start to see you as more than just the person who sends them a large bill every month. They might even start to think of you as a friend of sorts. And trust me, friends are far more forgiving than clients. If something goes wrong on their file, or you need to have a tough conversation, they'll be far less likely to go all rabid Pitbull on you. Instead, they'll remember the pleasant chats and the fact that you actually care about them as people.

Let's be clear: this isn't about manipulating your clients. It's about genuinely caring and showing interest in their lives. People can tell the difference between fake niceties and genuine interest. Be authentic. If you're genuinely interested in your clients, they'll sense it, and the relationship will be stronger for it.

Now, a word of caution. While building a personal connection is important, maintain professional boundaries. You don't need to know every detail of their personal lives, and they don't need to know yours. Keep the conversation light and steer clear of sensitive topics. You're still their lawyer, not their therapist.

Making a personal connection with your clients can transform your professional relationships. It's a small investment of time and effort that can lead to significant rewards. Your clients will see you as a trusted advisor and a friend, making the tough times easier to navigate. So, next time you're meeting with a client, take a few minutes to chat about their latest vacation or their favorite sports team. You'll be surprised at how far a little personal connection can go. And who knows, you might even enjoy these conversations as much as they do.

# Bad Instructions

Here is one of the more delightful aspects of practicing law: bad instructions from clients. You know, those moments when a client insists on something that makes you want to bang your head against your desk. Maybe they want you to write a scathing letter that will accomplish nothing except inflaming the situation. Or perhaps they want you to take a ludicrous position in court that has about as much chance of success as a snowball in a sauna. Or they insist on making an insulting offer that you're certain will torpedo any chance of a reasonable settlement. The joys of client management.

Here's the good news: most clients, when presented with your sage advice, will see the light and back down from their ill-advised positions. After all, they hired you because you're the expert, and they're not. But what do you do when they won't budge?

First and foremost, having a client who doesn't follow your advice is not good. It's like having a backseat driver who insists on taking the wheel while you're navigating a hairpin turn. Remember, they hired you because you have the expertise they lack. They should not be the ones driving the car.

Secondly, consider the potential damage to your reputation. Following bad instructions might tarnish your standing with opposing counsel or the court. And in the world of law, your reputation is your most valuable possession. Guard it as though your livelihood depends on it—because it does. A single client's unreasonable demands are not worth risking the professional respect you've worked so hard to earn.

So, what do you do when a client insists on bad instructions? My advice is to politely but firmly explain that you don't feel comfortable following their instructions because they are against your professional judgment. Let them know that if they insist on taking that course, they should find a different lawyer to handle their matter. This isn't just about protecting your reputation; it's about maintaining your integrity and ensuring that you're providing the best possible service.

Dealing with bad instructions from clients is part and parcel of being a lawyer. The key is to manage these situations with a blend of firmness and diplomacy. Protect your reputation, stand by your professional judgment, and don't be afraid to let go of clients who refuse to listen to reason. Remember, you're the expert—they hired you for your wisdom and experience, so don't let them steer you into the rocks.

# Talk About Fees Early and Often

One of the most important tasks that come with being a lawyer is discussing fees with your clients early in the process. Picture this: you've just wrapped up a complex case, and you send off the final bill with a flourish. Moments later, your phone rings, and your previously cheerful client sounds like they've just discovered their favorite coffee shop has doubled their prices. Nobody likes being surprised with a big bill they weren't expecting, and your clients are certainly no exception.

To avoid this drama, make it a point to talk about fees early and often. Think of it as one of those awkward but necessary conversations, like explaining to a roommate why they need to clean the dishes before they start growing their own ecosystem. From the very outset, be crystal clear about your fees, how you bill for your time (yes, those friendly emails and quick phone calls count), and provide an expected range for the services they're asking you to provide. Transparency is your best friend here.

When you first meet with a client, lay all your cards on the table. Explain your hourly rate, how you track your time, and what they can expect in terms of billing. For example, let them know that a 15-minute phone call is not just a pleasant chat but a billable event. It's better they know upfront that every interaction is part of the meter running, much like a taxi ride.

But don't stop there. Break down the process into stages and give estimates for each stage as it arises. Suppose they want you to go to court for an application. In that case, provide them with a clear estimate of the expected cost and confirm their instructions before proceeding. This isn't just about good client relations; it's about protecting yourself from the dreaded "But I didn't know it would cost this much!" conversation.

One thing I've found particularly effective is to provide regular updates on costs as the matter progresses. It's like sending a mid-trip text to someone who's waiting for you—keeps them in the loop and prevents them from worrying about where you've disappeared to. A simple email or call to say, "We've spent X amount so far, and we're on track to spend Y for the next stage," can do wonders for client trust and satisfaction.

Another consideration is whether a flat fee makes sense for the matter you're working on. Flat fees can be a godsend, both for you and your client. They remove the element of surprise when the final bill arrives and allow your client to budget accordingly. Plus, if you've been diligent (and I know you have, because you're reading this book), you'll already have the agreed amount in trust, making the final transaction smooth and stress-free.

Talking about fees early and often is crucial to maintaining a healthy and transparent relationship with your clients. By setting clear expectations from the beginning, providing estimates at each stage, and considering flat fees where appropriate, you can avoid the unpleasant surprise of an outraged client. Remember, clear communication about fees is essential for a harmonious and successful legal career. So, go forth and discuss those fees with confidence and clarity—you and your clients will be better off for it.

# Legal Advice for Family and Friends

One of the unpleasant discoveries you'll make early in your legal career is that every single person you've ever met—your aunt, your high school buddy, your neighbor who you only exchange awkward waves with—will suddenly have a pressing legal issue they want your help with. You'll find yourself navigating a minefield of personal and professional boundaries, and how you handle these situations can make all the difference.

If it's something non-contentious, like drafting a will or handling the purchase of a home, go ahead and lend a hand. These tasks are straightforward, and the risk of ruining a relationship is minimal (but not non-existent). Plus, it's a great way to build goodwill. But when it comes to high-conflict matters, you need to tread carefully. Ask yourself: Are you prepared to lose this person in your life if things don't go their way?

Consider the emotional and time investment. High-conflict matters are called high-conflict for a reason—they can drain you both emotionally and physically. Before you jump in with both feet, think about how much time it will take and whether you're willing to offer a substantial discount or do it pro bono, aside from disbursements. Be wary of offering too much and finding yourself mired in a case that consumes countless hours and a good chunk of your sanity.

Let me share a little nugget of wisdom: aside from simple transactional matters, the best approach is often to provide some general advice and then refer them to a lawyer you know will take good care of them. You can explain, with genuine regret, that you value their friendship too much to risk it by handling this emotionally charged event. They might be disappointed at first, but they'll appreciate your honesty and your commitment to preserving your relationship.

And here's a fun fact, one that seems to be written in the stars: if you do take on a matter for a family member or friend, anything that can go wrong probably will. It's just one of those laws of the universe, like gravity or the inevitability of finding your keys in the last place you look. So, prepare yourself for the unexpected, and don't say I didn't warn you.

Remember, your time is valuable, and so are your relationships. Balancing the two can be tricky, but with a thoughtful approach, you can navigate these waters successfully. By providing general advice, referring out more complex cases, and setting clear boundaries, you can help your friends and family without risking your personal relationships.

Handling legal requests from friends and family is an art form. Approach it with care and consideration. By managing expectations and knowing when to say no, you'll maintain your relationships and your peace of mind. And remember, sometimes the best way to help is to know when to step back.

# Section 5: Practice Management and Efficiency

# The Whiteboard

As a junior lawyer, you'll find yourself in the wonderful (but sometimes awful) position of being everyone's go-to person for projects. Seriously though, this is fantastic for gaining experience across various areas, but it can quickly turn into a juggling act that makes the circus look like a piece of cake. How do you manage the flood of tasks and know what to prioritize? Simple: get due dates on projects and make them visible.

Here's what I suggest: invest in a big, glorious whiteboard and hang it prominently on your office wall. Not only will this make you look impressively organized, but it will also become your new best friend in managing your workload. Every time a new task lands on your desk, ask the assigning lawyer for an expected completion date. Then, jot down the task, its due date, and the name of the lawyer who assigned it on the whiteboard. This isn't just for your benefit; it's a visual cue for everyone else who walks into your office.

Here is how it works: Lawyer A comes in with a new research project and sees your whiteboard filled with tasks, each with a due date. They immediately see that Lawyer B has already given you something due tomorrow, and Lawyer C has a project due next week. Instantly, they have a clear picture of your workload.

This little bit of transparency works wonders. More often than not, they'll adjust their expectations to fit into your existing schedule. It's like magic, but with dry-erase markers.

Despite their sometimes gruff demeanor, senior lawyers are usually nice people who genuinely want you to succeed. They remember their own days of junior lawyerdom and the mountain of tasks that came with it. By providing them with this information in an inoffensive and organized manner, you're helping them help you. It's a win-win situation.

Getting due dates on projects and displaying them prominently is a simple yet powerful tool for managing your workload as a junior lawyer. It keeps you organized, helps you prioritize, and provides transparency for the senior lawyers assigning you tasks. And remember, behind every great lawyer is a whiteboard filled with due dates.

# Skip Lunches Out…Within Reason

The lunchtime ritual is a beloved tradition where lawyers escape their desks, stretch their legs, and indulge in food that didn't come from a microwave. You'll quickly notice that some of your colleagues head out for lunch almost every single day. It's understandable. Lunch out provides a much-needed break, a chance to socialize, and probably a better meal than the sad sandwich you hastily threw together this morning. But let's talk about the dark side of these midday escapades: they're colossal time vampires.

Let's do the math. If you spend an hour to an hour and a half out for lunch each day, that's 5 to 7.5 hours a week – almost a full day's worth of billing. That's a significant chunk of your time—time that could otherwise be spent getting through your mountain of work or, more importantly, leaving the office at a decent hour. The legal profession is notorious for being demanding, so any strategy to reclaim your time should be welcomed with open arms.

This isn't to say you should skip every single lunch out. Far from it. Socializing with colleagues is essential. It builds camaraderie, allows you to network informally, and shows you're part of the team. Plus, if you skip every lunch, your colleagues might start to think you're not fun, or worse, stingy. We don't want that.

So, what's the solution? Moderation. I suggest picking one day a week to treat yourself to an out-of-office lunch. Fridays always feel like the right day for me—there's something about the end of the week that makes a leisurely lunch feel like a reward for surviving the daily grind. It's a nice way to unwind and recap the week with your peers.

Here's another tip: when you do go out for lunch, keep an eye on the clock. Try to keep it to an hour. This way, you enjoy the break without letting it devour too much of your day. Set a reminder on your phone if you have to.

For the rest of the week, consider bringing your lunch from home. It might not be as glamorous as dining out, but it's efficient and often healthier. Use this time to catch up on reading, prep for an afternoon meeting, or even take a quick stroll to get some fresh air and clear your mind.

Let's not forget the financial aspect. Eating out every day can be a drain on your wallet. By limiting your lunches out, you save money—money that could be better spent on something more enjoyable than a daily sandwich and soda.

Skipping lunches out—within reason—is a smart strategy for managing your time and maintaining a balanced work life. It's all about finding that sweet spot between being productive and staying connected with your colleagues. By treating yourself to an occasional lunch out, you keep the social benefits without letting it become a time-sucking habit. So, pack that lunch, enjoy your Fridays, and reclaim your afternoons.

# Rip the Bandage Off: Do Your Most Difficult Tasks First

Your to-do list will often resemble a battleground, with tasks vying for the title of "Most Unappealing." There always seems to be one particularly daunting task that feels more unappealing than all of the others. You know the one—the task that makes your stomach churn just thinking about it and causes you to lay awake at night. Maybe it's drafting a complex memo or application, or making a dreaded phone call to a client to deliver bad news. Regardless, the urge to procrastinate on these unsavory tasks is enormous.

I'm here to tell you that you need to tackle these tasks first thing when you walk into the office. Think of it as ripping off a bandage—sure, it might sting a bit, but the relief that follows is worth every bit of discomfort.

Here's why this strategy is so effective. When you do the most difficult task first, you set a positive tone for the rest of your day. You've conquered the mountain before breakfast, and everything else on your list seems like a gentle stroll through the park. Imagine the satisfaction of having that massive, anxiety-inducing task checked off your list by mid-morning.

Conversely, if you put off the daunting task, it will fester in your mind, growing more monstrous and terrifying with each passing hour. It's like the monster under the bed—it gets scarier the longer you avoid looking at it. By tackling it head-on, you eliminate the mental dread that saps your energy and focus.

Now, a word of caution. Some tasks might require more time and resources than you initially anticipate. That's okay. The key is to start. Break the task into manageable chunks if you need to, but make sure you tackle the hardest chunk first.

Adopting the "rip the bandage off" approach to your most difficult tasks is a game-changer. It reduces stress and boosts productivity. So, next time you walk into your office and see Taskzilla lurking, don't run away. Charge at it with gusto, rip that bandage off, and enjoy the sweet, sweet relief that follows.

# Bill Every Single Month

Billing is the not-so-joyous task that ensures we get paid for our hard work. Yet, let's be honest, it really does kind of suck. It typically involves a couple of hours of tedious labor: going through your bills, correcting errors, deciding on any appropriate discounts, and comparing what you initially estimated versus what you actually billed. In short, it's the kind of task that makes you wish you were doing almost anything else, preferably something that's actually billable work. But despite its tedium, billing is a necessary evil that must be done every single month.

I've seen far too many lawyers fall into the trap of procrastinating on their billing. Maybe they think it's easier to wait until the file is over, or perhaps they're anxious about how the client will react to that first bill. Trust me, don't fall into that trap. Staying on top of your billing is a crucial duty you owe to your clients and, let's face it, to yourself.

First, why billing sucks. There's nothing particularly thrilling about sifting through time entries and expenses and debating whether a client will balk at the amount you've billed. It's a bit like cleaning out the garage: necessary, but hardly the highlight of your week. However, think of billing as a monthly maintenance task, like changing the oil in your car. It might not be fun, but it keeps everything running smoothly.

One of the main reasons you must bill every single month is to keep your clients informed. Regular billing ensures that your clients know exactly where their money is going and what the financial tally is to date. It's all about transparency. Imagine a client receiving a massive bill at the end of a long project. They're likely to be shocked, outraged even, because they weren't expecting it. Regular, monthly billing helps manage their expectations and prevents unpleasant surprises.

Moreover, regular billing is vital for your financial health. It's what keeps the lights on, the coffee flowing, and food on your table. In the hustle and bustle of legal work, it's easy to forget that you're running a business. And like any business, cash flow is king. Waiting until the end of a project to bill can create gaps in your cash flow, leading to unnecessary stress and financial strain.

While billing may never be your favorite task, it's an essential part of your practice. By staying on top of your billing each month, you keep your clients informed, ensure steady cash flow, and avoid the pitfalls of procrastination. So, embrace the suck, get it done, and enjoy the peace of mind that comes with knowing your financial house is in order.

# Keep Track of Time Concurrent with Work

Timekeeping is an unglamorous yet essential part of a lawyer's life. You have a nifty piece of software that's designed to make your life easier and the most critical aspect of this tool is your timesheet. This is where you'll record every single 0.1 of your working life. My advice? Keep track of your time concurrent with your work.

I have a colleague who, despite all logic and reason, insists on entering the entirety of her time once a month. Picture her the evening before billing day, huddled at her desk for hours, sifting through emails and phone call notes, trying to piece together her time for the month like a detective reconstructing the scene of a crime. Honestly, I don't know how she does it. You don't want to be her. Let her be a cautionary tale of what not to do.

Now, let's get into the nitty-gritty of why you should enter your time as soon as you complete a task. For starters, it ensures accuracy. Imagine trying to remember how long that conference call with Bob the Builder took three weeks ago. Was it 0.4 hours or 0.6? The details blur, and suddenly, your best guess feels more like a shot in the dark. By entering your time immediately, you capture every minute accurately, ensuring you don't miss any billable moments. And let's be honest, every 0.1 counts when you're on the clock.

Keeping track of your time throughout the day also prevents the monumental task of month-end time reconstruction. Instead of facing a Herculean effort to recall every email, phone call, and meeting, you spend a few seconds here and there inputting your time. Small, manageable steps lead to less stress and a much clearer picture of your productivity.

Keeping track of your time concurrent with your work is not just a good habit; it's essential for your sanity and efficiency. It ensures accuracy, saves you from end-of-month timekeeping marathons, and helps maintain a clear record of your productivity. So, take a few moments after each task to log your time. Future you will thank present you for the foresight and organization.

# Staying Organized: To-Do Lists and BF Systems

In the whirlwind world of law, where multitasking is a daily requirement and deadlines loom like menacing storm clouds, keeping organized is essential for survival. Enter the humble to-do list and the slightly more sophisticated bring forward system (BF System).

First, let's talk about the to-do list. Imagine it as your personal command center, a place where all your tasks are neatly laid out, waiting to be conquered. Your to-do list can take many forms: a whiteboard on your wall (highly recommended for reasons previously discussed), a piece of paper on your desk, or an electronic list on your computer or smartphone. The format is less important than the habit of maintaining it.

Why is a to-do list so critical? For one, it keeps you focused. In a profession where you're constantly juggling multiple matters, it's all too easy for something to slip through the cracks. Imagine you're deep into drafting a complex motion when a client calls asking for an update on another matter. You scramble through your mental files and realize you've forgotten something crucial. The to-do list prevents these mini heart attacks by ensuring you always know what's on your plate.

Your list should include the task, the assigning lawyer (if applicable), and the due date. This way, you have a clear snapshot of what needs to be done, who's waiting for it, and when it's due. And trust me, there's no better feeling than crossing something off that list.

Now, onto the BF System. It's an internal system, usually managed by your assistant, designed to keep track of due dates for everything under the sun—court filings, client follow-ups, deadlines for responses, and more. The BF System is your safety net, ensuring that no critical date slips by unnoticed.

Get your assistant to explain how your firm's BF System works and make sure you understand it inside and out. This system is your best friend when it comes to avoiding missed deadlines, which not only make you look bad but could also result in disciplinary action or even lawsuits. Yes, it's that serious.

Maintaining a to-do list and mastering your BF System are essential tools for keeping your professional life in order. Your to-do list keeps you focused and gives you the joy of crossing off completed tasks, while the BF System ensures that no critical deadlines are missed. Together, they form an organizational powerhouse.

# Pro Bono Work

You're a newly minted lawyer with a shiny new degree and bar admission - you're ready to take on the world. But wait—here come the invitations and requests to provide your services for free. Yes, pro bono work will start to crop up like weeds in your garden of billable hours. You'll be invited to sit on boards, offer free legal advice at community centers, and give presentations to various organizations. Pro bono work is an altruistic endeavor, and I encourage all lawyers to find a way to give back to the community. But be careful not to take on too much.

Let's start with why pro bono work is important. We are in a privileged position where we have been granted the right to practice law and earn a good income as part of a self-regulated profession. Many people cannot afford our services and should not be allowed to slip through the cracks. Doing pro bono work is not only about giving back but also about ensuring access to justice for everyone, regardless of their financial situation. Plus, it feels good to help someone in need.

Now, let's address the practical side of things. Your initial instinct might be to say yes to every pro bono opportunity that comes your way. After all, you're enthusiastic, eager to help, and maybe a little afraid of saying no. But before you know it, you've taken on the equivalent of a second or even third job with your pro bono commitments. This is where the trouble starts.

You need to be smart about how you manage your pro bono work. Start by setting a limit on the number of hours per week or per month that you feel comfortable committing to. This is crucial. Think of it as setting a budget for your time. Just as you wouldn't spend all your money on one thing, you shouldn't spend all your time on pro bono work, no matter how noble the cause.

Next, be selective about the organizations you choose to work with. Make sure they align with your passions and interests. If you're passionate about housing rights, find an organization that focuses on that. If you're interested in environmental law, look for opportunities in that field. This way, you're more likely to stay motivated and less likely to feel resentful about the time commitment.

Think of pro bono work as a side dish to your main course of billable work. You want a balanced plate, not one overflowing with mashed potatoes. A little bit goes a long way, and it's the variety that keeps things interesting and sustainable.

Pro bono work is an essential part of being a responsible lawyer and giving back to the community. But it's important to balance these good intentions with the realities of your workload and personal life. Set clear limits on your pro bono hours, choose causes you're passionate about, and remember that it's okay to say no sometimes. By doing this, you'll be able to contribute meaningfully without burning out.

# Screen Your Calls

Let's talk about being good at multitasking, that beloved myth we all like to believe in. The truth is, everyone's productivity plummets when trying to juggle multiple matters at the same time, especially when we're interrupted every five minutes. One of the easiest ways to derail a productive morning is to answer a random phone call that throws you completely off task. It could be a client with a minor issue or, heaven forbid, a cold call. Either way, it's time to set up a system to prevent these interruptions.

Here's where your trusty assistant comes into play. The first point of contact for anyone trying to reach you should be your assistant. They're like your personal gatekeeper, shielding you from distractions and ensuring your focus remains intact. This is how you maintain your productivity.

Imagine this: You're deep in the zone, drafting a complex motion or preparing for a crucial meeting. Suddenly, the phone rings. It's a client who wants to discuss the weather, their pet's health, and oh, maybe a minor legal query that could have waited. There goes your train of thought, derailed and scattered to the winds. By the time you hang up, you've lost precious minutes, if not hours, trying to get back on track.

Now, picture this instead: Your phone doesn't ring. Your assistant fields the call, handles the minor query, and schedules a time for you to speak with the client about the more significant issue. You remain blissfully uninterrupted, powering through your tasks with the efficiency of a Swiss watch.

Setting up this system is straightforward. First, sit down with your assistant and establish clear guidelines for call screening. Define what constitutes an emergency and what can wait. Empower your assistant to handle queries within their capacity. Many times, a client's question is something your assistant can address without needing to disturb you.

For instance, if a client calls asking about the status of a document or the next steps in a routine process, your assistant can provide the information. If it's something more complex or sensitive, they can schedule a call at a time that fits your schedule. This way, you get uninterrupted work periods and can batch your calls together, addressing multiple issues in one focused time slot.

Additionally, consider setting specific times of the day for returning calls. Let your clients know that you're available for calls between, say, 3 PM and 4 PM. This not only helps manage your time but also sets clear expectations for your clients.

Think of your assistant as the bouncer at an exclusive club, with you being the DJ spinning the hits (or in this case, drafting the hits). The bouncer ensures that only the most crucial guests get through to you, keeping the riff-raff at bay. This way, you can keep the party going without any unnecessary interruptions.

Screening your calls is a simple yet effective strategy to boost your productivity and keep your sanity intact. By setting up a system with your assistant as the first point of contact, you can focus on your work without constant interruptions. Your productivity will skyrocket, and you'll find yourself more in control of your time. Embrace the power of call screening and enjoy the peace and efficiency that comes with it.

# Manage Your Appointment Times

As a new lawyer, one of the most critical skills you'll need to master is managing your appointment times. Imagine running from one appointment to another, trying to squeeze in bathroom breaks, and wondering when you might actually sit down for a meal. Chaos, right? But it doesn't have to be this way. Properly managing your appointment times is one of the keys to maintaining your sanity and productivity.

For me, the golden hours for appointments are 10 AM and 2 PM. Why, you ask? It's all about balance. Scheduling appointments at these times ensures that I have ample time with each client while leaving myself enough time to tackle other tasks, like drafting documents, preparing for court, and yes, going to the bathroom and eating.

My advice is to limit yourself to a maximum of two appointments per day. This might sound overly cautious, but there are good reasons for this. With only two appointments, you can dive deep into each matter without feeling rushed. You can listen, advise, and strategize without constantly glancing at the clock. And it gives you those precious blocks of uninterrupted time to get significant work done.

But what about those days when you need to hunker down and focus? Don't be afraid to block off days for no appointments. These are your sacred days for tackling significant work that requires no interruptions. Mark them on your calendar and guard them fiercely.

Of course, there will always be exceptions to your carefully crafted schedule. Urgent matters will arise, and preparing for court appearances might drag your appointment times into the evening or weekend. It's the nature of the beast. But for the most part, clients will quickly learn your preferred times and will stick to them. People are surprisingly accommodating when they know what to expect.

Now, let's talk about a common dilemma: the potential new client who insists they can't make it during regular business hours and prefers evening or weekend appointments. Here's a piece of advice that will save you some grief: you don't want those clients. Politely decline and advise them that you only set appointments during regular business hours. If they're unwilling to accommodate your schedule, they're likely to be a source of future problems.

Managing your appointment times is about finding balance and maintaining control over your day. By scheduling appointments at set times, limiting the number per day, and blocking off no-appointment days, you can create a manageable and productive work environment.

# Section 6: Practice Tips

# How to Deal with Difficult Opposing Counsel

You will find a rich tapestry of personalities—some delightful, others less so – in the legal profession. Unfortunately, our field seems to attract more than its fair share of difficult people. While most lawyers will fight hard for their clients while still being courteous and respectful, you will inevitably encounter those who treat every conversation like a war and who skate perilously close to ethical boundaries. These characters are well-known in the legal community, and you'll quickly learn who they are from your colleagues. Here's how to handle them with grace and professionalism.

First and foremost, never, ever stoop to their level. You aren't a jerk, and you don't need to become one to get the job done. Always be courteous in your communications, even when they are not. Imagine you're a Zen master, maintaining your calm while the storm rages around you. This not only keeps you sane but also earns you respect from judges and other professionals who witness your demeanor.

Consider the medium of your communication carefully. Difficult opposing counsel can turn a simple phone call into a verbal battlefield. If you find that every phone conversation leaves you seething or if they're habitually disrespectful, insist that all communications be in writing. This isn't about being difficult yourself; it's about creating a clear, documented trail of interactions. Plus, written communication tends to be more measured and thoughtful, which is precisely what you want in contentious situations.

There's another reason to keep things in writing: integrity. If you question their honesty or suspect they might misrepresent conversations, having everything documented is a lifesaver. Written records protect you and your client and can be invaluable if disputes arise about what was said or agreed upon.

When responding to their inflammatory correspondence, channel your inner Vulcan—be factual and impassionate. Remember, every letter you write has the chance of being read by a judge. You want to look like the reasonable, composed lawyer, while letting the other lawyer look like a deranged lunatic. Your goal is to maintain professionalism and focus on the issues, not get dragged into a personal mudslinging contest.

Finally, seek support from your colleagues. Venting to a trusted coworker or mentor can provide much-needed relief and perspective. They've likely dealt with similar characters and can offer valuable advice and reassurance. Plus, it's always nice to know you're not alone in facing these challenges.

In conclusion, dealing with difficult opposing counsel is an unfortunate but inevitable part of the legal profession. By maintaining your professionalism, insisting on written communications when necessary, and responding factually and unpassionately, you can navigate these encounters effectively. Remember, your reputation as a reasonable and courteous lawyer is one of your greatest assets. Protect it fiercely, and let the difficult ones paint themselves into their own corners.

# Use Alternative Dispute Resolution Tools

Welcome to the fascinating world of Alternative Dispute Resolution (ADR), a toolkit of strategies designed to help you resolve your client's matters more quickly, more cost-effectively, and with more privacy than the traditional court route. I believe you'll find ADR to be an invaluable asset in your legal arsenal. Typically, lawyers think of mediation and arbitration, but I consider any meeting or communication for settlement purposes to be ADR. Let's dive into why ADR should be your go-to method whenever possible.

Firstly, let's talk about mediation. Mediation is essentially a negotiation with a referee. The parties and their lawyers gather with a mediator—often an experienced lawyer or retired judge—who helps facilitate discussions and steer the parties towards a mutually acceptable resolution. Even when parties seem locked in their positions, it's amazing the compromises that surface during mediation. People are funny that way; sometimes all it takes is a fresh perspective and being face-to-face to get them to budge. It's astonishing how quickly disputes can dissolve with the right guidance.

Settlement discussions fall under the ADR umbrella as well. Every time you have the parties together—whether in a meeting, a hallway outside a courtroom, or even during a court recess—view it as an opportunity to discuss settlement options. These informal talks can often lead to breakthroughs that formal negotiations miss. I've resolved numerous cases through conversations at the courthouse or during examinations or depositions. Always be prepared for these opportunities. Keep settlement options at the forefront of your mind, and don't be shy about bringing them up unless it's clearly inappropriate.

One of the biggest advantages of mediation and settlement discussions is the cost savings for your clients. Litigation is expensive, time-consuming, and emotionally draining. If you can resolve a matter through a negotiated settlement, you're saving your client money, time, and stress. Even if you think there's little chance of resolution, it's usually worth trying. The potential savings and the possibility of a quicker, more amicable resolution make it an option that's hard to ignore. Also, your clients control the outcome with this approach instead of leaving it in a stranger's hands.

Now, let's move on to arbitration. Arbitration is a private trial conducted by an experienced lawyer or retired judge. It's particularly helpful when the parties want to avoid the often-overbooked court system or keep their private affairs out of the public eye. Think of it as the VIP lounge of legal disputes—exclusive, efficient, and away from prying eyes. Be careful, though, as arbitration can cost more than the traditional court route since you need to pay for the decision-maker's time and the venue.

A final word on ADR: tailor your approach to the specifics of each case. While ADR is suitable for many situations, it's not a one-size-fits-all solution. Evaluate each case on its own merits and consider whether ADR is appropriate. In my experience, there are few cases that don't lend themselves to some form of ADR.

Embrace ADR as a powerful tool in your practice. Whether through mediation, arbitration, or informal settlement discussions, ADR can often achieve outcomes that are just as satisfying as those reached through litigation, but with far less hassle. So, next time you're faced with a contentious matter, remember that there's a world of alternative dispute resolution out there, ready to make your life—and your client's life—much easier.

# You Will Make Mistakes…That's OK

In the world of law, the standard we often hold ourselves to is nothing short of perfection. We lawyers, along with our clients, frequently expect a flawless performance. Here's a bit of reality: perfection is a myth. Mistakes will happen—especially as a junior lawyer. The sooner you accept this, the healthier and more productive your career will be.

As a new lawyer, you're like a fledgling bird awkwardly flapping around, trying to find your wings. You're going to make mistakes. The good news is that mistakes become less frequent as you gain experience, though you will never eliminate them completely. And that's okay. Learning to live with the fact that you're not perfect—and neither is your staff—is crucial.

When a mistake happens (notice I say "when," not "if"), the best course of action is to address it immediately. Don't let it fester like a week-old sandwich forgotten in the back of the fridge. Acknowledge that a mistake was made and take steps to remedy it as best you can. Own up to it. No excuses, no hiding, just a straightforward admission of error. This approach not only demonstrates integrity but also helps you maintain credibility with your clients and colleagues.

When you make a mistake, take the time to analyze what went wrong and why. Was it a lack of communication? Did you misinterpret something? Understanding the root cause will help you avoid similar mistakes in the future. Keep a journal or a log of these lessons learned—it might sound tedious, but it's incredibly valuable for your growth.

Don't blame others. Imagine you've just discovered that you missed a critical filing deadline. Panic sets in. Your first instinct might be to point fingers, perhaps blame your assistant for not reminding you. Resist that urge. Blaming others, especially in front of clients or the court, makes you look unprofessional and undermines your authority. Remember, you are ultimately responsible for every mistake on your file, regardless of who made it.

Never throw your assistant or other staff members under the bus. Clients and judges don't want to hear excuses about why something isn't your fault. They want to know what happened and how you're going to fix it. Taking responsibility shows that you're reliable and that you stand by your team.

Think of your mistakes as stepping stones in the river of your legal career. Yes, you might get your feet wet or even fall in a few times, but each stone helps you get to the other side. Every mistake is a learning experience. The more you learn, the better lawyer you become.

Lastly, remember to cut yourself some slack. Perfection is an unrealistic expectation. You're human, and humans err. What matters is how you handle those errors. Face them head-on, learn from them, and move forward.

Making mistakes is an inevitable part of your journey as a lawyer. Embrace them as opportunities for growth rather than reasons for despair. Address mistakes promptly, take responsibility, and learn from each one.

# Talk to a Practice Advisor

Wouldn't it be wonderful if the legal world were simply a set of black-and-white rules? Unfortunately, it's not. Instead, we live and work in a world of ambiguity and vagueness, where many situations don't come with a clear right or wrong answer. As a new lawyer, you'll encounter challenging scenarios where the path forward is murky at best.

You might find yourself tangled in a tricky ethical dilemma, torn between your duty to your client and your duty to the profession. Or perhaps a mistake was made on a file, and you're at a loss for how to handle it. When these moments arise—and they will—it's crucial to know that you don't have to navigate them alone.

In my jurisdiction, our Law Society provides Practice Advisors to assist in these perplexing situations. It's likely that your Law Society offers a similar service, and you should make it a point to familiarize yourself with it. A Practice Advisor is typically an experienced lawyer who can provide sage advice on these thorny issues.

When you find yourself in a sticky situation, one of the first step is to contact your Practice Advisor. They can help you navigate ethical dilemmas, procedural uncertainties, and even those moments when you've made an error and aren't sure how to proceed. At best, they'll guide you through the minefield. At worst, it will be noted that you sought and followed advice from a Practice Advisor if things go south.

Here's an example: Imagine you've discovered a potential conflict of interest in a case you're handling. The rules seem vague, and you're not sure whether you need to disclose it or withdraw from the case altogether. This is a perfect moment to call your Practice Advisor. They can provide clarity and suggest the best course of action, potentially saving your bacon (and your reputation).

Beyond resolving specific issues, talking to a Practice Advisor can also serve as a learning experience. Each conversation with them adds to your reservoir of knowledge, helping you become a more competent and confident lawyer.

Now, you might think that reaching out for help makes you look weak or inexperienced. Let me assure you, it doesn't. Seeking advice when needed shows wisdom and a commitment to ethical practice. It demonstrates that you're thorough, conscientious, and dedicated to doing things the right way.

Don't hesitate to talk to a Practice Advisor when you're faced with challenging situations. They are a valuable resource, offering guidance and support when you need it most. By leveraging their expertise, you'll navigate the gray areas of law with greater confidence and skill. Remember, even seasoned lawyers consult with Practice Advisors—so consider it part of your ongoing professional development.

## Listen: Really, Stop Talking So Much

There are days when I wonder if the art of listening is a lost art, especially in the legal profession. Look, I know you have lots of really important things to say—pearls of wisdom, witty retorts, and brilliant insights. But let me give you a piece of advice that might just change your life: zip the lips and open the ears and you will be a better lawyer.

When meeting with clients, the best service you can provide initially is a pair of attentive ears. Let them tell their story. Let them pour out their grievances, hopes, and every little detail they think is important. This does two things: it makes them feel heard and valued, and it gives you a wealth of information. In our profession, information is a valuable commodity. You can't gather information if you dominate every conversation. Plus, there's nothing clients appreciate more than feeling genuinely listened to.

Here's a practical tip: ask open-ended questions. This encourages clients to share more details and nuances about their situation. Questions like "Can you tell me more about that?" or "How did that make you feel?" are gold mines for gathering insights. Remember, you're not just collecting facts—you're understanding your client's motivations, fears, and desires. This deep understanding is what allows you to craft the best legal strategy for them.

Let's talk about senior lawyers. They've been around the block, seen it all, and have a treasure trove of wisdom to impart. When a senior lawyer is sharing their experiences, resist the urge to interject with your own stories or opinions. Listen carefully to every single word. These nuggets of wisdom can save you from making rookie mistakes and can provide invaluable lessons that you won't find in any textbook. Plus, it shows respect for their experience and knowledge, which can only help in building a good rapport with your senior colleagues.

Listening is also crucial in the courtroom. Every single word that a judge says is important. Judges don't babble—they make points that can determine the outcome of your case. Listen attentively, take notes, and never assume you already know what they're going to say. This attentive listening can provide you with the insights needed to adjust your strategy on the fly.

Here's another secret weapon: silence. Most people feel uncomfortable with silence and will rush to fill it with words. When people babble, they often say more than they intend to, revealing information that can be incredibly useful. By remaining silent, you encourage others to keep talking, providing you with even more information. This doesn't mean you should be a stone-faced mute, but strategic silence can be a powerful tool.

The art of listening is not just a nice-to-have skill; it's essential for your success as a lawyer. By listening more than you speak, you gather invaluable information, build stronger relationships, and avoid the pitfalls of babbling. So, zip those lips, open those ears, and embrace the power of listening.

# Go to Court as Much as Possible

The courtroom—a place where legal theories meet the real world and where every lawyer's mettle is truly tested. As a new lawyer, you'll discover that courtroom experience is invaluable, and there are certain things that simply can't be taught in a classroom. There are myriad procedures and customs to learn, from the straightforward—like where to sit and how to address the judge—to the more complex, such as making objections or impeaching a witness. The best way to learn these intricacies is to dive in and get into court as much as possible.

Courtroom procedures can seem daunting at first, but they become second nature with practice. Knowing where to sit, how to introduce yourself, and the appropriate ways to address the judge and opposing counsel are fundamental skills that set the stage for everything else you'll do in court. These might seem like minor details, but they form the foundation of courtroom etiquette and professionalism.

One of the best ways to start gaining courtroom experience is to accompany senior lawyers from your firm. If your firm has senior lawyers who regularly go to court, approach them and ask if you can tag along. This is a golden opportunity to observe and assist them on their matters. Maybe you can handle the questioning of a particular witness or draft materials that will be used in court. Or perhaps your role will be more modest, like carrying their bags and taking notes. No matter the task, every bit of exposure to the courtroom environment is invaluable.

Court work is an art form, and while you'll eventually develop your own style, it's essential to learn by watching the experts in your field operate. Observe how they handle themselves, how they interact with judges and opposing counsel, and how they structure their arguments. Take notes—literal or mental—about what works and what doesn't.

If you don't have senior lawyers to take you to court, don't despair. Make time to go to court and observe on your own, even if it's just once a week or every other week. Watch how different lawyers present their cases, what the judges seem to appreciate, and the common pitfalls to avoid. It's a bit like auditing a masterclass—there's much to be learned from simply watching and listening.

When the opportunity arises for you to appear in court on your own, seize it with both hands. Yes, it can be intimidating, but the earlier you have your first appearance in front of a judge or your first solo trial, the better. The longer you wait, the more terrifying the prospect will become. Embrace these opportunities as they come. You'll learn more from one morning in court than from weeks spent poring over textbooks.

Immerse yourself in courtroom experiences as much as possible. Whether you're assisting a senior lawyer or observing from the gallery, each visit to the court adds to your practical knowledge and confidence. When it's your turn to stand and deliver, you'll be prepared and poised. Remember, every great lawyer started as a novice, and the courtroom is where you truly hone your craft. The more you do it, the better you'll become.

# Don't Specialize Too Early

Specializing in one or two areas of law is a great idea. It allows you to become an expert in your field and avoid the headache of learning new areas with every client. However, it's nearly impossible to know which area will be the most interesting and rewarding for you until you've dabbled in a variety of fields. This is why I suggest you gain broad exposure to multiple areas of law during your first couple of years of practice.

Imagine the start of your legal career as a visit to an all-you-can-eat buffet. You wouldn't pile your plate high with one dish before sampling the rest, would you? Of course not. You'd try a bit of everything until you find what you really like, and then you load up on that. The same principle applies to your legal practice.

You might start with a passion for transactional work because the thought of public speaking makes you break out in a cold sweat. But after a few courtroom appearances, you could discover a hidden zeal for criminal law that makes you feel like a modern-day Perry Mason. Conversely, you might dream of being a star litigator, only to find that you get immense satisfaction from drafting a really solid will. (Okay, that last scenario is a bit of a stretch, but you get my point.)

Exploring different areas of law has several advantages. First, it broadens your skill set. The more areas you experience, the more versatile and adaptable you become. You'll find that many legal matters overlap into different areas, and having a broad knowledge base allows you to say, "Hey, I know how that works!"

Second, it gives you a better understanding of what you enjoy and where your strengths lie. Law school can give you a taste of various fields, but practicing law is a whole different ball game. You won't truly know what resonates with you until you're in the trenches, dealing with real clients and real cases.

Third, it makes you more marketable. Firms appreciate lawyers who have a well-rounded background. It shows that you're flexible and willing to step out of your comfort zone. Plus, having experience in multiple areas can make you a valuable asset to a team handling complex, multifaceted cases.

Take your time to explore different areas of law before you decide to specialize. Treat your early years as a lawyer like a visit to a legal buffet. Sample a bit of everything, discover what you enjoy and where your strengths lie, and then focus on those areas. You'll become a more well-rounded, adaptable, and fulfilled lawyer.

# Welcome to the Real World: Think Before You Act

Welcome to the real world, where the practice of law is far more nuanced than winning cases with brilliant legal arguments. In the trenches of legal practice, the decisions you make can have profound, real-world consequences. As you embark on your legal career, let me impart some wisdom: always consider the impact of your actions.

Too many lawyers fall short by not thinking through the ramifications of their decisions. Sure, drafting an angry letter might feel cathartic, but will it actually help your client's situation? Often, it can escalate tensions and make a bad situation worse. Imagine you're in a delicate negotiation, and you fire off a scathing missive. Suddenly, the other side is on the defensive, and the chances of a reasonable settlement go up in smoke.

Take a moment to consider: will this course of action make things better or worse? The real world isn't as clear-cut as a law school casebook. You must balance the legal strategy with the practical realities your clients face.

Consider your client's mental and emotional state. Clients aren't just case files; they're real people with real stresses and anxieties. Is your client mentally prepared to go through a grueling trial, or would they be better off with a lesser settlement that provides more immediate peace of mind? Sometimes, securing a swift, less lucrative settlement is far more beneficial than winning a larger sum after years of litigation. A client who emerges from a trial financially victorious but emotionally drained might not thank you for your courtroom heroics.

Remember, the goal isn't to win at all costs; it's to achieve the best possible outcome for your client. And that "best outcome" isn't always measured in dollars and cents. It's measured in the client's overall well-being, the preservation of relationships, and the minimization of stress and expense.

Think of your legal actions as a game of chess, not whack-a-mole. In chess, every move is calculated, with an eye on the entire board and several moves ahead. In whack-a-mole, you're just reacting, smacking down whatever pops up without any broader strategy. Be a chess player, not a mole-whacker.

In the real world, legal decisions ripple outward, affecting not just your client, but their family, their business, and their future. So, take a deep breath, step back, and think before you act. Consider the broader consequences.

The transition from law school to legal practice involves shifting your mindset from winning arguments to achieving the best practical outcomes for your clients. This requires a keen awareness of the real-world consequences of your actions. By considering the broader impact, you'll not only become a more effective lawyer but also a more trusted and valued advisor to your clients. Welcome to the real world, where thoughtful consideration and strategic thinking reign supreme.

# Section 7: Personal Well-Being

# The Sphere of Crisis: Keeping Your Sanity Intact

The best piece of advice I ever received about personal well-being in the legal field came during my first week of practice. A wise senior lawyer looked me in the eye and said, "Most of our clients are experiencing some sort of crisis that has led them to us, and they will do everything they can to drag us into their sphere of crisis." In other words, your distressed clients will want you to be just as distressed about their situation as they are. Don't be.

As a lawyer, you'll encounter clients with serious problems. They'll come to you with tales of woe, and they'll want you to join them in their emotional roller coaster. Here's the thing: their personal problems are not your personal problems. Your job is to solve their legal issues, not to take on their emotional baggage. Dealing with their problems is your job, not a personal crusade for justice.

Of course, we can all get a bit wrapped up in our clients' issues—that's inevitable. You wouldn't be a good lawyer if you didn't care at least a little. But when your clients' crises start preventing you from enjoying your out-of-office hours, it's time to take a step back. If you don't, you'll become mentally overburdened.

Taking on 40 or 50 clients' problems as your own is a surefire recipe for burnout.

Think of it this way: if you were a firefighter, you wouldn't bring the fire home with you. You'd extinguish it at work and leave the soot and ashes behind. Similarly, as a lawyer, you need to address your clients' crises during office hours and then leave them at the office door.

Imagine your client's crisis as a wild, thrashing octopus. It's your job to wrangle the octopus, but you don't have to invite it to dinner. Keep that octopus firmly in its tank and don't let its tentacles creep into your personal life.

To keep the octopus at bay, set clear boundaries. This might mean not answering non-urgent client emails or calls outside of work hours. Inform your clients upfront about your availability. Trust me, most of them will respect your boundaries if you clearly communicate them. For those who don't, a gentle reminder usually does the trick.

Additionally, develop healthy coping mechanisms. Exercise, hobbies, and spending time with loved ones are excellent ways to decompress. These activities help you recharge and maintain your sanity. Remember, you can't pour from an empty cup. Taking care of yourself isn't just good for you; it's also in the best interest of your clients. A well-rested, mentally healthy lawyer is far more effective than a stressed, burned-out one.

While it's natural to care about your clients and their issues, it's crucial to maintain a healthy distance. Your clients' crises are not your own. By setting boundaries, developing healthy coping mechanisms, and delegating tasks, you can keep their crises from consuming your life. Remember, your primary role is to provide legal solutions, not to become entangled in their emotional turmoil. Keep the octopus in its tank, and you'll navigate the turbulent waters of law with your sanity intact.

## Guard Your Personal Time

Hear me loud and clear on this issue: the practice of law will consume the entirety of your life if you allow it to. There's always one more file to review, one more email to send, one more call to make. It really never ends, and you might wish you could multiply yourself at times. Despite this, it's of paramount importance to your personal health that you maintain a life outside of the law. Here's how you do it.

First and foremost, set boundaries. Don't take appointments in the evenings or on weekends unless absolutely necessary. Your time outside of work is just that—your time. Protect it fiercely. Similarly, don't check your work email in the evenings or on weekends unless it's a genuine emergency. And let me tell you, most things can wait until the next business day. The world won't implode because you didn't reply to an email at 9 PM on a Saturday.

Now, let's talk about the sacred art of taking holidays. Plan regular, real holidays where you completely check out. I'm not talking about a long weekend where you're still peeking at your phone every five minutes. I mean a proper vacation, where your assistant isn't calling you twice a day and you aren't checking emails from a beach lounger. You need a chance to recharge your batteries.

Think of yourself as a smartphone. If you don't recharge, you'll end up with about as much functionality as a brick. You need that downtime to refresh and rejuvenate. Burnout isn't just a catchy term; it's a very real consequence of not giving yourself adequate breaks.

Now, I can hear some of you thinking, "But what if something urgent comes up?" That's where a bit of planning and delegation comes in. Ensure your assistant and colleagues know you're taking time off well in advance. Set up an out-of-office reply for your email, directing any urgent matters to a trusted colleague who can handle things in your absence. Believe it or not, the legal world can turn without you for a week or two.

While we're on the subject, let's talk about the benefits of taking these breaks. Besides the obvious (not feeling like a zombie), taking time off improves your productivity and creativity. You'll return to work with a fresh perspective, more energy, and perhaps even a few new ideas. Plus, you'll be more pleasant to be around, both in the office and at home.

Guarding your personal time and taking real holidays are essential to maintaining your sanity and effectiveness as a lawyer. Set boundaries, unplug completely during your breaks, and delegate responsibilities while you're away. Remember, you can't pour from an empty cup. By taking care of yourself, you'll be better equipped to take care of your clients. So, go ahead—book that vacation, and let the law take care of itself for a little while. Your future, well-rested self will thank you.

# Exercise, Maintain Hobbies, Eat Well

Believe me, lawyer butt is a real thing. Five years into my legal career, I found myself 25 pounds heavier and huffing and puffing with every flight of stairs I had to climb. I was overweight, out of shape, and generally unhealthy. So, how did this happen? I wasn't making my physical and mental health the priority it should be. It's easy to convince ourselves that we no longer have time for things like exercise and hobbies, but this couldn't be further from the truth.

Let's start with exercise. I know, I know—you're busy. You have clients to meet, briefs to write, and a never-ending stream of emails to answer. But here's the thing: you need to make time for exercise. Buy an exercise bike (this is what I did) or go for a walk instead of a lunch out. You don't need to become a marathon runner or a CrossFit enthusiast, but you do need to move. Make it a priority to get 30 to 45 minutes of exercise every single day. Schedule it in your calendar just like you would a client meeting.

Now, let's talk about hobbies. Remember those things you used to do for fun before you started drowning in a sea of legal documents? Whether it was playing soccer, attending a book club, painting, or even collecting Pokémon cards, you need to keep doing them. Hobbies provide a much-needed break from the grind and help maintain your mental health. They remind you that there's more to life than billable hours and court appearances.

Now, onto food. Ah, the siren song of greasy burgers and fries, calling you from the depths of your stress-induced hunger. While there's nothing wrong with indulging occasionally, greasy burgers shouldn't be a staple in your diet. Eating well is crucial to maintaining your energy levels and overall health. If you find that you don't have time to cook healthy meals for yourself during the week, consider getting meal kits delivered. They're a lifesaver and ensure you're eating balanced, nutritious meals without the hassle of meal planning.

In addition to exercise and hobbies, don't underestimate the power of social connections. Spend time with friends and family, engage in community activities, and build a support network. It's easy to get tunnel vision in the legal profession, but having a strong support system can provide perspective and encouragement when things get tough.

So, let's recap: make exercise a non-negotiable part of your day, maintain the hobbies that bring you joy, and eat well. These practices will make you a happier, healthier person, which is good for your clients, your family, and your colleagues. And who knows? You might even inspire some of your fellow lawyers to join you on this journey to better health.

# Reward Yourself Because Nobody Else Will

After the 20-plus years of schooling you've endured to get to this point, saying you're accustomed to being evaluated and rewarded for good work is likely an understatement. From the earliest grades, where gold stars adorned your papers for keeping your desk clean or correctly reciting the twelve months in order, to the final days of law school, eagerly awaiting confirmation that you aced that Securities exam, you've been conditioned to expect recognition for your achievements. Well, welcome to the world of practicing law, where such affirmations are as rare as a unicorn in a courthouse.

In your new role, you'll draft brilliant legal memos that never get read, deliver incredible oral arguments in court only to be met with a mute, frowning judge, and secure amazing settlements for your clients who then complain about their bills. It's a world where your hard work and dedication often go unnoticed. So, what do you do when nobody seems to want to give you the gold star you so richly deserve? Simple: you reward yourself.

The key to maintaining your sanity and motivation in this often thankless profession is to become your own cheerleader. Celebrate your victories, no matter how small they may seem. Did you finally get that reluctant client to agree to a reasonable settlement? Treat yourself. Did you survive a grueling week of depositions and court appearances without a single meltdown? That's worth celebrating.

Let's start with some tangible rewards. Buy yourself a piece of clothing you've had your eye on or a new gadget that makes your heart sing. Maybe it's a sleek new bike or those noise-canceling headphones that will make your commute a little more bearable. The act of gifting yourself something tangible creates a physical reminder of your hard work and success.

But don't stop there. Consider experiences that allow you to unwind and recharge. Treat yourself to a massage or a spa day. Imagine lying on a massage table, the soothing music playing softly in the background, while all the stress knots in your shoulders get expertly kneaded away. Pure bliss, right? Or perhaps a nice dinner out with your partner or friends, where you can enjoy good food and great company, away from the stacks of legal briefs and the constant ping of emails.

The specific reward doesn't matter as much as the act of acknowledging your accomplishments. The point is to make rewarding yourself for your victories a priority. This practice is crucial for your mental well-being. It's a way of telling yourself that your hard work matters, even if the outside world doesn't always acknowledge it.

The legal world may not always offer the recognition you deserve, but that doesn't mean you should go without. Rewarding yourself is an essential part of maintaining your morale and motivation. So, celebrate your victories, big and small, and remember that you're doing a great job, even if nobody else says so. After all, you've earned it.

# Beware of Substance Abuse and Mental Health Issues

This is a somber topic to address to end this book, but it is also perhaps the most important piece of advice in this book. The statistics are stark: lawyers experience significantly higher levels of substance abuse and mental health issues than the general population. It's a reality that casts a shadow over our profession, and one that we must confront head-on.

Being a lawyer is inherently stressful. The pressure to perform, the high stakes of our work, and the often adversarial nature of the job can take a toll on anyone. Unfortunately, not everyone copes with this stress in healthy ways. I've seen several lawyers face personal and professional turmoil due to substance abuse issues. I've witnessed colleagues driven from the profession entirely because of mental health issues. This isn't just an abstract concern—it's a very real danger.

First and foremost, be aware of these risks. The demands of legal practice can lead to long hours, high anxiety, and a relentless drive for perfection. It's easy to fall into unhealthy habits. The occasional drink to unwind can spiral into a dependency. The stress relief found in substances can become a crutch. The isolation from the long hours can deepen into depression.

Recognize these dangers early and take proactive steps to manage your stress and mental well-being.

Let's talk about prevention. Maintaining a healthy work-life balance is crucial. Make time for exercise, hobbies, and social activities outside of work. Seek out supportive relationships, both personal and professional. Don't neglect your physical health—eating well and getting enough sleep are fundamental. And most importantly, don't bottle up your stress. Talk to friends, family, or a professional about what you're experiencing.

If you think you may have a problem with substance abuse or mental health, seek help immediately. Your Law Society will have confidential resources available to assist you. These services are there to support you, and taking advantage of them is a sign of strength, not weakness. Remember, you're not the first lawyer to face these issues, and you won't be the last. The sooner you seek help, the better the outcome will be.

Finally, be vigilant not only for yourself but for your colleagues as well. If you see a colleague struggling with substance abuse or mental health issues, reach out to them. Offer a listening ear, encourage them to seek help, and support them through their journey. Sometimes, knowing someone cares can make all the difference.

While the legal profession is demanding and stressful, it's essential to prioritize your mental health and well-being. Be proactive in managing stress, seek help when needed, and support your colleagues.

# Conclusion

As you close this book and take your first steps into the exhilarating, challenging, and rewarding world of legal practice, I want to extend my heartfelt congratulations and best wishes. You have chosen a path that is as demanding as it is fulfilling, a profession that will test your mettle and reward your perseverance.

Remember, the journey you are embarking on is not just about mastering the law, but about growing as a person and a professional. You will face obstacles and triumphs, stress and satisfaction, late nights and celebratory moments. Embrace each experience, learn from every challenge, and never stop striving to be the best version of yourself.

As you embark on this journey, I hope you carry with you the lessons and wisdom shared in this book. They are not merely tips for surviving the rigors of legal practice, but guidelines for thriving and finding fulfillment in your work.

May you find success, satisfaction, and joy in your practice. Remember, the law is not just a profession but a calling, one that has the power to make a significant difference in the lives of others.

Welcome to the world of law, and best of luck on your journey. May it be as rewarding and enriching as you have always hoped it would be.

Sincerely,

Taylor S. Prescott

www.ingramcontent.com/pod-product-compliance
Lightning Source LLC
Chambersburg PA
CBHW050104230526
45470CB00004B/1668